WARNING

THIS BOOK MAY BE EXTREMELY
DANGEROUS TO THE LIFE EXPECTANCY
OF A POOR, TIRED, ANEMIC WORKLIFE.

The
PERFECT
RESUME
for the '90s

TOM JACKSON

The Perfect Resume

DOUBLEDAY

NEW YORK LONDON TORONTO SYDNEY AUCKLAND

PUBLISHED BY DOUBLEDAY
a division of
Bantam Doubleday Dell Publishing Group, Inc.
666 Fifth Avenue, New York, New York 10103

DOUBLEDAY and the portrayal of an anchor
are trademarks of Doubleday, a division of Bantam Doubleday
Dell Publishing Group, Inc.

This book is dedicated to a purpose: *To expand people's*
ability to bring who they are into the work world,
in a way that produces satisfaction and aliveness for them,
and value for others.

ISBN 0-385-26745-2
Library of Congress Catalog Card Number 79–7802
Copyright © 1981, 1990 by Tom Jackson

Contents

To Rewrite a Book
on Resumes

When the first edition of this book was written—in the now distant '70s—it was clearly a labor of urgency. The new thinking about how people could make the most of their best by taking initiative in managing their own career development and job searches was fresh and exciting, and the move to take the ideas and processes of job search out of the hands of traditionalists and institutions and give it to individuals themselves was active and very relevant. The urgency we felt was based on the, then, lack of good advice for job seekers about how to present their best on paper. The first job was to rush new ideas and examples to the population as quickly as possible.

For this task we must still send thank-yous to Ruth Gutstein, Audrey Hagemaier Sloofman, and Kevin Lane, the original resume team.

Today, as we go to press with the book's first major revision, after helping with hundreds of thousands of high-impact resumes, we have the luxury of a more career-savvy reader base. Today's resume has different challenges to meet: technology and entrepreneurism, global changes in market, services and products, calls for the articulation of subtler tones, more sophisticated examples, new uses for word processor and computer.

In helping to fine-tune both examples and style, we add to our resume honor roll Jerry Lee, master of word processor; Carole Bell, pursuer of esoteric career futures; and, as always, supporter of the perfection available to all of us: Ellen.

This book is a product of our commitment to you, the reader and user.

Tom Jackson
New York City, 1989

The 1990s: An Era of Career Challenge

As we approach the twenty-first century A.D., it is essential to take a fresh look at our relationship to careers, jobs, and the way we manage our work-lives. The current decade, born of the tremendous structural, humanistic, and technological changes of the '70s and '80s, already demonstrates a unique dynamic with important implications for your personal success, fulfillment, and prosperity. There is some good news, and some not-so-good news.

UNCERTAINTY FACTORS

As a career/life strategist you first need to be aware of the many uncertainties that will powerfully influence personal tactics and outcomes. To navigate through the shifting rocks and shoals that lie ahead, you must learn more sophisticated career game plans. The broad generalizations that satisfied past generations are not sufficient guidance for today's predictable unpredictability.

Without doubt, we will continue to experience the gale strength interplay of national and multinational stock market forces that can redefine entire corporate cultures virtually overnight, mindlessly knocking over hundreds of well-prepared career paths with a flick of financial leverage. Global politics will set in place both competitive and protectionist movements that challenge old markets and hegemonies. A unified European marketplace is but one example.

The shift away from goods-producing industries will continue, and by the global year 2000 nearly four out of every five jobs will be in the service-producing industries. You need to pay attention to this and what it means.

Hard numbers may not be as important as leadership qualities and creativity. The fastest growth will be in managerial, professional, and technical fields, requiring strong ongoing education and training.

BRAIN WAVES

The demand for knowledge and skills is insatiable. Tech-knowledge is required even for those of us who aren't technologists. If you don't know how to build it, you must certainly know how to put it to use. Or—equally valid—know how to learn how to deal with what's new. The learning lines merge in computers, automation, communication, electronics, health care, entertainment, space exploration, solar power generation, and fast food . . . plus all those things that will surface by this time next year that we can't imagine today. Lifetime learning is in to stay. How and where this shows up on the resume is important to you.

THE CAREER ENTREPRENEUR

The entrepreneurial perspective is a significant force in the work economy, and something to be kept in mind by every job seeker. Career entrepreneurship—marketing yourself as a value-added "product"—requires different resume approaches than traditional career-pathing. New job creation—a function of changing interplay between technology and economy—will continue unabated. The next job you have may not even be named today. Your top-playing resume will emphasize versatility and endurance.

Opportunity is exploding, and you can be the beneficiary. New opportunities to discover and solve local, national, and planetary equations are there for the asking. There is enough variety now for a great many of us to design the careers games we want to play . . . so long as we remember that what we build, we may need to change or discard.

As career entrepreneurs, we want more autonomy and choice. We seek jobs in which change, flexibility, and variety are expected. Many will choose a personally exciting job over one that is simply high-salaried. Job contracts are being rewritten: permanent part-time, consultant, free-lance, contracted, or at-risk. New options abound!

In the midst of all this, a shift in values is also evident. Intangibles are becoming increasingly important—the focus is on self-expression, self-fulfillment, and wellness. Human potential is popular again.

THE LIVING RESUME

Given the dynamics of this explosive new age we work in, it is almost inevitable that you will make about ten important job moves with perhaps three or four complete changes in direction by the time you are fifty-five.

You might go from media planner to program designer to telemarketer, or from minister to career counselor. There is no prescribed "up" direction you need to follow. No position is intrinsically better or more fun than another. Weaving this all together in the resume is an exercise in marketing, and this time you know the product well.

The perfect resume is the one that gets you one-on-one with the career decision-makers you plan to meet, a resume that stays on line and keeps growing: it works for you; you don't work for it! The perfect resume has several faces; it is not boxed in by job title. Clearly there is no one best way to write your resume, except the way that works for you right now.

Enjoy this book, which is dedicated to your exciting career future.

How to Use This Book

This book is a resource for you and has been designed to be used and not just read and digested. Its purpose is to assist you in putting together the best possible personal statement of your skills, abilities, and accomplishments in a way that will motivate employers to want to see you and to want to discuss employment possibilities.

Depending upon where you stand in your career—how much you have already done to prepare yourself—you will need or want to use different parts of the book to write a perfect resume for yourself. Shown below are three alternative ways to get the best from this volume.

THE *VERY* SHORT COURSE

If you are already very *clear about your job target* or work direction, and have had *good prior experience with resumes,* and feel confident in your writing skills, you can effectively prepare your resume by hitting the following key stepping-stones in the book. This will save you hours.

1. Remind yourself of the underlying principles of an effective resume. Read pages 5–10.
2. Read pages 39–48 about job targeting and complete page 48.
3. Select the resume format that best represents you—after reading pages 52–57.
4. Use the appropriate resume drafting tools for the format you have chosen. See pages 71–112 for directions.
5. Review sample resumes. See Resume Selector on pages 136–141.
6. Perfect your resume in Step 5, pages 112–117.
7. Write a perfect cover letter using the method on pages 117–121.
8. Brush up on job-hunting skills, pages 205–209.

THE SHORT COURSE

If you are very certain about your job target or work direction but unsure about how to effectively represent that in your resume, follow this simple path:

1. Learn the underlying principles of the perfect resume. Read Inside the Executive Suite, pages 5–10.
2. Read pages 39–48 and fill in your job targets on page 48.
3. Read and do Preparing the Perfect Resume, pages 49–117.
4. Review sample resumes. See the Resume Selector on pages 136–141.
5. Prepare a perfect cover letter, pages 117–121.
6. Brush up on your job-hunting skills, pages 205–209.

THE FULL COURSE FOR THE '90S

If you are ready and willing to take a fresh look at possible work directions, or if the idea of work that represents both skills and interests intrigues you, and if you are also interested in investing a small but important amount of time in building the perfect resume for yourself, you are in exactly the right place at the right time—this entire book is for you.

Find yourself a comfortable place to work. Get out the pencils and paper. Heat up the coffeepot and the word processor. Start at the upper left of the next page and work your way through to our perfect-resume ending.

THE CAREER DISCOVERY PROCESS

We are happy to be able to include in this book a completely separate section designed to assist in one of the most difficult tasks most people face in their worklives: selection of satisfying career directions and job targets.

This process is the culmination of many years of development and thousands of individual and group counseling sessions and workshops. The discovery process is designed to go beyond the usual vocational aptitude approach, into a deeper realm of personal awareness and understanding in a way that can be translated into the pragmatic reality of tomorrow's work world.

You do not *need* to do this process in order to create a great resume, but know that you will find it to be valuable and expanding.

AND MORE ...

In the closing pages we have included a distillation of some valuable job-finding tips that will help speed you, perfect resume in hand, into the opportunities of your choice.

Attention computer users: *The Perfect Resume Computer Kit™* allows you to work interactively with the materials in this book on any PC or Macintosh. Using this software, you can customize your resume automatically to meet the needs of many employers. The cost of this powerful software is under $50. For a free brochure write Permax Systems, PO Box 6455, Madison, WI 53716. To order by phone: (800) 233–6460.

Happy surfing and cheers!

PRELIMINARIES

INSIDE THE EXECUTIVE SUITE

Consider this: Roger Dupre, the employment manager of Aspect Publishing, a Midwestern firm specializing in sales promotional graphic systems, has had a rotten day. He started late due to a flat tire discovered just as he was about to leave for work. Frustration mounted when he got to work and found his parking place taken by an unknown vehicle and, after circling the lot twice, had to park three blocks away.

That was just the beginning—things continued downhill: two unexpected meetings, a dozen unavoidable phone calls, materials late from the printers, an angry manager with a labor grievance.

And, to top it all, his boss visited late in the day complaining that the CAD/CAM Group still hadn't seen any applicants for their three new job openings.

Roger held his breath and counted to ten when his boss left, lowering his blood pressure a few points and allowing his pulse rate to ease back from red alert. Roger has been here before and knows that there was no easy way to circumvent the problems. He buzzed his secretary: "Hank, it's another one of those days, I'm afraid, except worse. Pat was down asking about those openings we got last week from the CAD/CAM Group. She'd had a complaint from the department because they haven't seen anyone. I don't know why they're complaining so soon. We just got the openings, didn't we?"

"Well, not exactly," he replied. "We actually got the orders two weeks ago. We've run an ad in the *Trib* and alerted the agencies."

"But what's happened—have we gotten any response? I haven't seen anything."

"Oh, yes," he replied. "We've had an overwhelming response. From our ad alone we've gotten over a hundred resumes, and dozens more from the agencies. You told me to hold the responses and you would go over them when things calmed down. I probably should have reminded you, but you've been so busy. I'm sorry."

Roger didn't know whether to laugh or cry. On one hand, it was good to know that there was something to work with to fill the openings. On the other hand, he shuddered and his eyes teared at the thought of going through all those resumes. No wonder he had conveniently forgotten about the openings.

"Okay, Hank—do me a favor. Ask Phyllis to put them all in a box. I'll take them home and read through them tonight when I have a little peace and quiet. Next time, don't let me put this stuff off."

Later, with his son in bed and his late supper downed, Roger sets out to review the aspirations and careers of 152 job candidates for three positions. The task is formidable: every resume and every letter is different—from one-page handwritten notes, to a twelve-page laser-printed "personal presentation."

Most of what he reads is irrelevant and poorly organized. Long sentences and paragraphs run on without pause or punctuation. Some are just bare-bones outlines of job titles, spanning dozens of years of work but without a hint of accomplishment or results produced. Roger's mind goes on vacation. His analytical judgment is short-circuited by the task of simply reading the information, let alone relating it to the company's needs.

Document by document, he sorts the papers into two stacks: *Consider Further* and *Reject*—the basic geometry of the employment-screening process. Later, he will take the *Consider Further* pile and sort through these resumes again. Then he'll make further cuts, rejecting those that don't grab his attention. Despite his promise to himself to look through the rejects again, he won't get around to them, and in a week or so their authors will all get polite turn-down letters.

Roger has fallen into a pattern that is repeated every single day by thousands of employers involved in the screening process. Without being aware of it, and faced with a virtually impossible amount of raw, unorganized, nonstandard resume data, he has opted for the now-standard initial "screening out" process, which has become largely the measurement not of the abilities and accomplishments of the candidates but *the quality of the resumes themselves.*

To restate this: Because employers are obliged to sort through large volumes of nonstandard resumes, they resort to screening them initially on the basis of the quality and clarity of the resumes themselves, rather than on the inherent qualities of the candidate. This means that well-qualified people often are not considered for positions, due to poor resumes. It also means that, by developing good resumes, less qualified candidates will greatly improve their chances of being interviewed and receiving offers.

WHAT IS THE PERFECT RESUME?

The perfect resume is a written communication that clearly demonstrates your ability to produce results in an area of concern to selected employers, in a way that motivates them to meet you.

Be willing to analyze that description with us further. It reflects the basic philosophy of this book. The key concepts:

COMMUNICATION

The essential ingredient in communication, from our point of view, is personal responsibility. The definition we use is this: *Real communication is being responsible (100 percent) to ensure that a message is received.* This means that if the reader doesn't get it, you didn't communicate. As simple as that. You don't get to blame the other guy. Habitually, most of us approach noncommunication by blaming someone else. "He never listens to me." "They're too dumb to understand this." "They never told me." These are common responses to the noncommunicative environment in which we live. They deny our responsibility in the matter.

The excitement of being responsible for your communication creates a livelier game. You discover ways to improve your effectiveness. You attract more truth from others and use it to improve yourself. In using this book, you are exercising responsibility for the effectiveness of your resume.

CLEARLY DEMONSTRATE

The resume does more than describe. By the way it is put together, it actually *shows* the reader how you do things. At one level it demonstrates how well you have mastered written communication—a key part of almost every valuable job these days.

At another level, the resume is a personal presentation of how you think of yourself. It is almost an axiom in career counseling that what the employer thinks of you ends up being pretty close to what *you* think of you. The resume quality demonstrates your self-appraisal.

At a final level, the resume, like your job campaign itself, demonstrates how you will get the job done. Your resume can be seen as a work project that you take on with yourself as the employer. How well you get the job done is available for all to see.

ABILITY TO PRODUCE RESULTS

At the bottom line, *results* count. Not reasons, not explanations, not excuses. Not even, for that matter, years of experience or education. The major question is, what happens after you start? What could *we* produce with you on our team? In a fast-moving, technologically oriented work world, yesterday's education and job may be irrelevant to the new problems that need to be faced. The resume is not your biography. *It is a prospectus for the future.*

CONCERN TO SELECTED EMPLOYERS

The resume is not the whole story. It is a directed communication to a particular audience: employers whom you have selected as meeting *your* qualifications.

Yes, we see *you* in the driver's seat in your career. You select job targets that represent the marriage of your own essential life interests, qualities, and skills—and project these job targets into the job market. The resume is designed to communicate specifically to that audience and to no other. If you have three job targets, you will have three different resumes. Home-based computer terminals multiply your options.

MOTIVATED TO MEET YOU PERSONALLY

The resume is not designed to get you the position. Sorry, but that's a fact of job life. The best that your resume will do for you is to get you in for the interviews and add some points on the scale for the final consideration. The perfect resume *will get you interviews* with employers who count by demonstrating that you have a valuable, potential contribution to make.

And a dividend. The purpose of the resume, as we discussed above, is to get you interviews with employers who meet your job target criteria. But there is another payoff, and that is to help you focus consciously on yourself and your worklife, to reconnect with where you are and where you want to go with your work. The very process of going through the material in this book will assist you in improving the quality of your worklife and, therefore, the quality of your life, since both are inextricably related.

TUNED TO THE '90s

Considering the economic, social, and technological complexities of the '90s, today's perfect resume needs to demonstrate all the features of a Swiss Army Knife and pocket computer modem to boot. The best resumes show versatility in both form and content.

Given the turbulence of the decade, for many firms the selected job candidate will look like an expert surfer: moving effortlessly among the waves and crosscurrents of change, always staying on top, allowing the sea change to energize effortless movement in new career dimensions.

This doesn't mean that all your straight-line experience needs to be slipped into a shredder. On the contrary, if you can demonstrate stability and versatility, experience and invention, survivorship and creativity, you could present the best of all. Examine what you've accomplished in a way that spotlights the uniqueness of your capacity to adapt to new, ever-changing challenges.

THE RULES OF THE GAME

Someone invites you over for a friendly game of cards, or backgammon, or football, or Trivial Pursuit. You accept. And when you turn the first card or roll the dice, or put the ball in play, one thing is probably a certainty. You and your co-players are all basically on the same wavelength about the ways the game is played. If not, you don't play. You wouldn't put a dollar down on a poker table unless you knew the rules. To do otherwise would brand you as a "sucker," in the impolite parlance of cardsharps.

All games have rules. The job game has rules. When you know the rules, you take away much of the confusion, mystery, and surprise.

This book is about the rules for resumes. It is also a book about winning strategies. Please don't put the biggest stakes you've got—your worklife— into the pot unless you know the rules of the game.

WHO NEEDS IT?

Most likely you do! Years ago resumes were associated primarily with professional people—educators, lawyers, professional managers, and the like. Now, in the '90s, with the emphasis on increased technology, flexibility, and change, the need for a resume extends through all white collar levels from executive to hourly workers, and to blue-collar and unskilled occupations as well.

Consider the entrepreneurial uses for a resume. You may prefer to start your own business or become a consultant as the best way to make a living in the work world. A power resume is used for fund raising or part-time work. A resume may be presented as part of a package to assist you in obtaining financing and in marketing your services to prospective clients.

Regardless of the level or scope of your work targets, a resume can benefit you. By putting yourself through the discipline of preparing the perfect resume, you will have greater clarity about your worklife purpose and will increase your ability to present yourself in a way that motivates employers to meet you.

It takes some work for you to do it. Which brings us to:

THE PAYOFF FOR YOU

The easy way to prepare a resume is to sit down with a pad of paper or at your PC or typewriter, start at the upper left-hand corner of the page, type or write down the facts and information as they occur to you until you get to the lower right, make a few corrections, have it retyped if necessary, crank out fifty copies or so on the local photocopy machine, put them in the mail, and then sit back and wait . . . and wait . . . and wait. Time to prepare: perhaps three hours. Time to wait for the right response: six to eight weeks—or longer.

In this book we have laid out a tougher path for you to follow. We have designed an approach that will move you out of novice class and on toward the higher rank of career professional.

Most of the book calls for your direct participation. By going through the entire perfect resume process we've outlined, you will have a resume in the top 10 percent of all job seekers. The cost to you in preparation time is perhaps ten to twenty hours. The payoff can be immense—three or four times the response from the employers *you* are interested in, and a more powerful selling tool in the bargain.

In cold hard cash alone, the value of a perfect resume is probably an additional 10 percent in your paycheck, due to the increased value of yourself that you have communicated.

In terms of increased potential for personal satisfaction in your work, the rewards are priceless. Hundreds of people who have used these procedures, have clarified their own interests and abilities and have learned how to prepare the best resumes, have enabled themselves to create their own job directions and achieved them. They have blazed a trail for you to follow. But watch out—there are pitfalls and personal barriers that can get in the way.

Pitfalls and Personal Barriers

Over twenty years of working with people in their job campaigns has taught us one very important lesson, which in our work has come to be called *the rule of inherent negativity*. It can be stated like this: *People very frequently fail to support their own best interests*. We know, in advance, that there will be many temptations for you not to follow the detailed steps outlined in this book *even though you believe them to be valuable for you*.

You may find yourself impatiently shortcutting from an earlier page in the book to a spot further along. This is a natural reaction to a subject that is as personal and introspective as creating a resume that really touches who you are. Please be prepared for the temptation to skip ahead, and know that your fertile mind will probably come up with a few excuses or reasons to explain or justify these jumps. See how many of these excuses you can identify in advance on the following checklist.

Excuses Checklist

Check any of the statements below that you feel might be used by you as reasons (real or imagined) or excuses to stop you from following the perfect resume process presented in this book:

_____ I don't have enough time to do all the preliminary stuff. I want a resume right away.

_____ I don't need to even look at my job targets. I already know what I want to do.

_____ Writing a resume is easy. This book complicates it.

_____ This book is not for people at my level—it's for those who are more educated.

_____ This book is not for people at my level—it's for those who are less educated.

_____ My old resume is good enough for me—after all, it worked before.

_____ I don't need a resume since I've never had any formal work experience.

_____ It's too complicated for me.

_____ It's too simple for me.

_____ I don't like a book that asks me so many questions.

_____ Why bother? There are no satisfying jobs for me out there anyway.

_____ I'm too old.

_____ I'm too young.

_____ I'm too lazy for this sort of thing.

_____ (You fill in) _____

_____ (You fill in) _____

However or whatever you answered above—or even if you didn't answer—*thank you* for staying with us so far and for participating in the perfect resume process. You may use as much or as little of this text as you care to or as, in your judgment, you find valuable. We don't require your doing all of it, and we *do* want you to give it a try.

TEN MOST COMMON RESUME WRITING MISTAKES

We've surveyed scores of prime employers, career counselors, and employment agencies to determine what they feel are the most commonly repeated mistakes in the thousands of resumes they see. Here they are:

1. Too long (preferred length is one page).
2. Disorganized—information is scattered around the page—hard to follow.

3. Poorly typed and printed—hard to read—looks unprofessional.

4. Overwritten—long paragraphs and sentences—takes too long to say too little.

5. Too sparse—gives only bare essentials of dates and job titles.

6. Not oriented for results—doesn't show what the candidate accomplished on the job—frequent platitudes disconnected from specific results.

7. Too many irrelevancies—height, weight, sex, health, marital status are not needed on today's resumes.

8. Misspellings, typographical errors, poor grammar—resumes should be carefully proofread before they are printed and mailed.

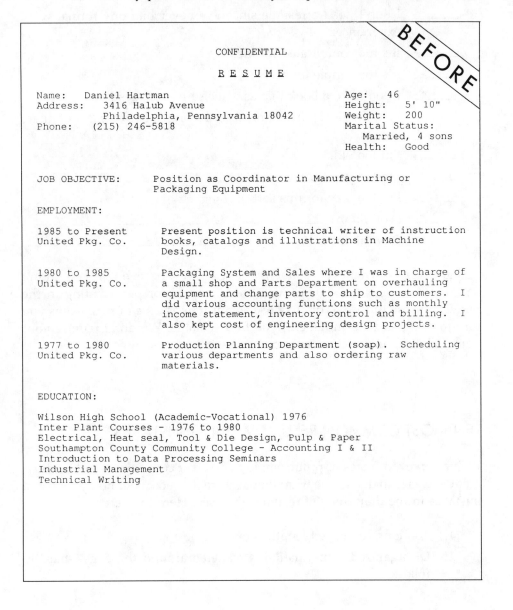

```
                        CONFIDENTIAL

                        R E S U M E

Name:    Daniel Hartman                    Age:    46
Address:    3416 Halub Avenue              Height:   5' 10"
            Philadelphia, Pennsylvania 18042   Weight:   200
Phone:   (215) 246-5818                    Marital Status:
                                               Married, 4 sons
                                           Health:   Good


JOB OBJECTIVE:      Position as Coordinator in Manufacturing or
                    Packaging Equipment

EMPLOYMENT:

1985 to Present     Present position is technical writer of instruction
United Pkg. Co.     books, catalogs and illustrations in Machine
                    Design.

1980 to 1985        Packaging System and Sales where I was in charge of
United Pkg. Co.     a small shop and Parts Department on overhauling
                    equipment and change parts to ship to customers.  I
                    did various accounting functions such as monthly
                    income statement, inventory control and billing.  I
                    also kept cost of engineering design projects.

1977 to 1980        Production Planning Department (soap).  Scheduling
United Pkg. Co.     various departments and also ordering raw
                    materials.


EDUCATION:

Wilson High School (Academic-Vocational) 1976
Inter Plant Courses - 1976 to 1980
Electrical, Heat seal, Tool & Die Design, Pulp & Paper
Southampton County Community College - Accounting I & II
Introduction to Data Processing Seminars
Industrial Management
Technical Writing
```

9. Tries too hard—fancy typesetting and binders, photographs and exotic paper stocks distract from the clarity of the presentation.

10. Misdirected—too many resumes arrive on employers' desks unrequested, and with little or no apparent connections to the organization—cover letters would help avoid this.

Before and After

On the previous page is a fairly typical resume of a job candidate who came to one of our workshops (all names and addresses have been changed in this book to protect the innocent—and the guilty!). Below is the resume produced after going through our processes.

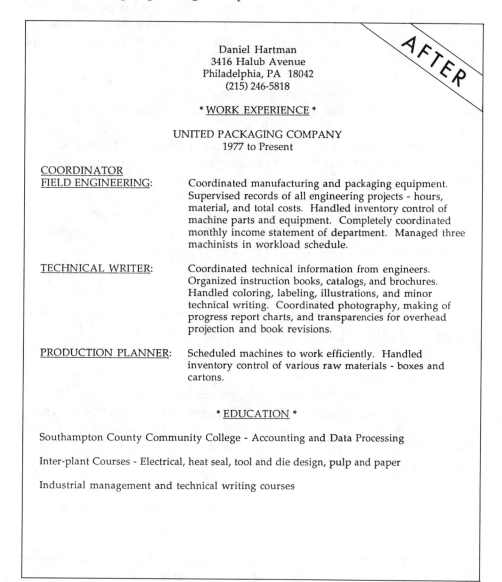

Daniel Hartman
3416 Halub Avenue
Philadelphia, PA 18042
(215) 246-5818

AFTER

* WORK EXPERIENCE *

UNITED PACKAGING COMPANY
1977 to Present

COORDINATOR
FIELD ENGINEERING: Coordinated manufacturing and packaging equipment. Supervised records of all engineering projects - hours, material, and total costs. Handled inventory control of machine parts and equipment. Completely coordinated monthly income statement of department. Managed three machinists in workload schedule.

TECHNICAL WRITER: Coordinated technical information from engineers. Organized instruction books, catalogs, and brochures. Handled coloring, labeling, illustrations, and minor technical writing. Coordinated photography, making of progress report charts, and transparencies for overhead projection and book revisions.

PRODUCTION PLANNER: Scheduled machines to work efficiently. Handled inventory control of various raw materials - boxes and cartons.

* EDUCATION *

Southampton County Community College - Accounting and Data Processing

Inter-plant Courses - Electrical, heat seal, tool and die design, pulp and paper

Industrial management and technical writing courses

THE CAREER DISCOVERY PROCESS

Years ago, when we first started to read and critique resumes for people, we kept running into a problem: the resume was not focused toward a particular job target or goal and, as a result, wandered rather aimlessly around the person's skills and abilities with little direction or clarity.

We discovered that, with a majority of clients, to start by assisting with the resume was like picking up a problem in the middle. We didn't have enough information to really help the job seeker present himself or herself in the proper focus. Hours would be required to address that persistent job seeker's lament: "I don't know what I want to do."

Over the succeeding twenty years of working on the front lines of the job search, we have devised and tested an evolving set of approaches to assist people in the discovery and definition of their career goals and job targets, which are of course followed by hard-hitting resumes that support and promote these goals.

In the next two chapters we have presented our current version of a personal process you can use to discover and reinforce your own career goals.

The Career Discovery Process is an important process and is not required if you are already very certain about your job targets and your skills and interests. If you want to move right into the resume preparation, you can skip to page 49 and go to work.

On the other hand, if you would like to explore, or re-explore, your basic skills and abilities and see how they fit into a satisfying job direction for you, we invite you to participate in the Career Discovery Process.

DEFINING YOUR MAGNIFICENCE

"The problem with most resumes is not so much the form of them, although that's bad enough, it's deeper than that. It's that the people who write them aren't really in touch with who they are—what they have to offer. Their magnificence, if you will. And it shows. Tell them not to rush into the resume right away. To sit back and take inventory first."

—Employment manager of
a multinational corporation

Yes, magnificence. Notice the resistance and doubt that surge forward at even the simple thought: Who me, magnificent?

The answer is yes, you. In your own particular configuration of skills, abilities, aptitudes, interests, energy, dedication, inspiration, and willingness to make a contribution, you are unique. Special. And perhaps you aren't in touch with that. Most of us aren't. It's much more common for people to focus on their insignificance, to be conscious of the things they can't do as well as someone else, to be controlled by their shortcomings. People invalidate themselves for what they aren't rather than appreciate themselves for what they really are.

Magnificence doesn't have a particular shape or form. It doesn't require outside approval or agreement. All it takes is the willingness to direct your attention to what you do have, rather than what you don't have—who you are, not who you aren't. Then, present this to the world with pride and certainty rather than apology and equivocation.

Here, in the Career Discovery Process, we are going to help you get in touch with the basic qualities and components from which to fashion your perfect resume—to uncover the primary sales points that will enhance your presentation to potential employers. We intend, in the process, for you to go beyond your own immediate self-image in order to see your value and significance to others, which you have probably taken for granted.

As most career counselors, psychologists, and employment experts will agree, self-analysis is one of the hardest things people have to face in organizing their job searches. The Career Discovery Process will make the task considerably easier.

YOU ARE NOT YOUR JOB TITLE (OR MAJOR FIELD OF STUDY)

If you have been working or going to school for a few years, by this time in your life you and the world have probably reached an agreement about what you are. You have, undoubtedly, temporarily satisfied the search for identity by assuming a work or professional title. After years of study you can now call yourself an engineer, or account executive or executive secretary, or broker or teacher, or career counselor. In short, you have pigeon-holed yourself, and it's comfortable.

The problem is that this approach to your worklife doesn't really support you very much. Every year, in our corporate career development work, we meet with countless men and women who have resigned themselves to their job titles, and surrendered their identities. We work with people who have lost touch with what they can do outside their job duties, who feel stuck with a narrow identity in a slot they lost interest in years ago.

Repeat: *You are not your job title*—you are, in fact, a versatile, many-faceted being with a storehouse full of qualities that can relate to a large range of work positions. Whether student or secretary, engineer or executive, you undoubtedly have a lot more going for you than you are willing to admit. Let's see how, together, we can dig some of this out.

THE BUILDING BLOCKS

As a human being you are endowed with, and have acquired, a large variety of personal and technical tools for dealing with the world around you. You have successfully developed thousands of routines or procedures for handling the day-to-day problems of life—*all* of life, from backyard to boardroom, from children to community, private life to professional life. These are your skills, abilities, and personal attributes. You wouldn't have made it this far if you didn't have them.

And, you have developed a pleasure profile, a shopping list of things that turn you on: puzzles that challenge you, sensations that tickle you, types of relationships that nurture you, environments in which you feel good, activities that contribute to your well-being and that of others.

All of the personal qualities, whether in the skill or interest family, can be seen as building blocks—elements from which you can fashion your job target of the moment. Now notice that, if you knock down the structure, remove the job title, you haven't lost anything: the building blocks are still there intact—all of them, including many you weren't using in the last job and perhaps forgot you had.

With knowledge of your personal building blocks, you can construct another job title, or target. And by being able to identify and describe these personal components, you will create the central core of your perfect resume. (Personal data, work history, and education will be added later.)

The Four Blocks

In the Career Discovery Process we analyze four primary building blocks that are very useful in your resume.

> BLOCK ONE—*Skills*
>
> BLOCK TWO—*Interests*
>
> BLOCK THREE—*Personal Attributes*
>
> BLOCK FOUR—*Results*

In the following pages you will explore each block or module separately, with exercises, checklists, and procedures designed to put you in touch with ways of communicating about yourself in effective resume terms. By participating in these exercises you will actually be writing this book with us, and the result will be *your* perfect resume, not ours.

Block One—Skills

There are two categories for you to look at here: *Basic Skills*, and *Specific Skills*. Basic Skills (writing, reading, driving, etc.) are the everyday foundations of our life in organized society and come primarily from early education. Many people tend to take these skills for granted, on the grounds that since "everyone can do this" why mention it? This is a mistake, as you will see.

Specific Skills (techniques) are the aspects of your abilities that most set you apart from others in your worklife. They are applications of your basic skills to the advancement of particular identifiable results. These techniques are not necessarily complicated or difficult; in fact they are normally fairly simple to describe. You may be surprised at the number you can come up with.

• Basic *Skills Checklist* •

Listed below is a cross-section of basic skills. Follow these instructions:

1. Read over the list, then check any skill box where you feel you have basic competence.
2. On the next page, add any other basic skills in which you are competent.
3. After you have gone over the list once, go back, and for each skill you have checked, indicate whether you would be willing to use this skill in your work.

• *Your* Specific *Skills (Techniques)* •

These skills are both job-related and non-job-related. They are things you have learned to do in school, on your own, or at work. The general criterion is that, when you apply the skill, a specific measurable *result* is produced.

Typing letters would qualify as a specific skill because the *result* (the typed letter) is there. So would designing bridges, planning sales promotion campaigns, farming, fund raising, etc. A good way to inventory specific skills is to start with a basic skill and add specificity. Thus, the basic skill of *writing* could translate to specific skills in:

writing reports
writing letters
writing stories
writing employee evaluations
writing travel itineraries, etc.

Competent	BASIC SKILLS	Willing to use in future work	Competent	BASIC SKILLS	Willing to use in future work
	Reading			Managing/Motivating Others	
	Writing			Remembering	
	Organizing			Classifying	
	Communicating			Innovating	
	Visualizing			Decorating	
	Selling			Working with Hands	
	Working with Numbers			Meeting Deadlines	
	Imagining/Creating			Making Decisions	
	Driving			Researching	
	Supporting Others			Keeping Records	
	Cooking			Working with Animals	
	Painting/Drawing			Performing	
	Learning Quickly			Conceptualizing	
	Traveling			Planning	
	Attending to Detail			Building	
	Dancing			Listening	
	Acting			Teaching Others	
	Performing Mechanical Tasks			Singing	
	Analyzing			Using Physical Dexterity	
	Operating Equipment			Entertaining Others	
	Working Outdoors			Using Tools	
	Counseling/Coaching			Growing Things	
	Investigating			Caring for Children	
	Negotiating				

List here any other basic skills you possess that we haven't included in our list above.

The basic skill of *analyzing* can be made more specific as:
    analyzing financial reports
    analyzing office problems
    analyzing work flow
    analyzing personnel requirements
    analyzing biological data

To start an inventory of your specific skills, review the list of basic skills you've checked off, and select the ten in which you feel most qualified and enjoy and are willing to use in your work. List each of the ten in one of the skill expansion boxes and complete the boxes in accordance with the following four specific instructions.

• Skill Expansion Boxes •

1. List each of the ten basic skills in one of the boxes provided on the following pages.

2. In each box list several other terms or expressions that are similar to the basic skill and write these related terms where shown below.

3. List at least five specific ways that you *could apply* (or have applied) these skills in work or nonwork activities. Don't limit yourself. Be expansive. You can edit later.

4. Keep going until you have at least fifty specific skills statements, then choose twenty of these statements to list in Skill Summary Sheet One on page 25.

SKILL EXPANSION BOX
SAMPLE

Basic Skill _____

Any other related terms which could describe this:

_____   _____

_____   _____

Specific ways in which I could apply this skill:

_____

_____

_____

_____

_____

SKILL EXPANSION BOX #1

Basic Skill _____

Any other related terms which could describe this:

_____   _____

_____   _____

Specific ways in which I could apply this skill:

_____

_____

_____

_____

_____

_____

SKILL EXPANSION BOX #2

Basic Skill _____

Any other related terms which could describe this:

_____   _____

_____   _____

Specific ways in which I could apply this skill:

_____

_____

_____

_____

_____

_____

SKILL EXPANSION BOX #3

Basic Skill _____

Any other related terms which could describe this:

_____   _____

_____   _____

Specific ways in which I could apply this skill:

_____

_____

_____

_____

_____

SKILL EXPANSION BOX #4

Basic Skill _____

Any other related terms which could describe this:

_____   _____

_____   _____

Specific ways in which I could apply this skill:

_____

_____

_____

_____

_____

SKILL EXPANSION BOX #5

Basic Skill _____

Any other related terms which could describe this:

_____   _____

_____   _____

Specific ways in which I could apply this skill:

_____

_____

_____

_____

_____

_____

SKILL EXPANSION BOX #6

Basic Skill _____

Any other related terms which could describe this:

_____   _____

_____   _____

Specific ways in which I could apply this skill:

_____

_____

_____

_____

_____

_____

SKILL EXPANSION BOX #7

Basic Skill _____

Any other related terms which could describe this:

_____   _____

_____   _____

Specific ways in which I could apply this skill:

_____

_____

_____

_____

_____

SKILL EXPANSION BOX #8

Basic Skill _____

Any other related terms which could describe this:

_____   _____

_____   _____

Specific ways in which I could apply this skill:

_____

_____

_____

_____

_____

SKILL EXPANSION BOX #9

Basic Skill _____

Any other related terms which could describe this:

_____   _____

_____   _____

Specific ways in which I could apply this skill:

_____

_____

_____

_____

_____

SKILL EXPANSION BOX #10

Basic Skill _____

Any other related terms which could describe this:

_____   _____

_____   _____

Specific ways in which I could apply this skill:

_____

_____

_____

_____

_____

Skill Summary Sheet One

Instructions:

1. Choose and list 20 specific skills (which are most valuable and enjoyable to you) from the Skill Expansion boxes. *It is not necessary to list them in priority order.*

2. After you have listed all 20, check the appropriate boxes to the right.

	I would enjoy performing this skill.	I consider myself to be qualified in this skill area.	I have actual work or nonwork experience in doing this.	This is something I would be willing to explore further.	
1.					
2.					
3.					
4.					
5.					
6.					
7.					
8.					
9.					
10.					
11.					
12.					
13.					
14.					
15.					
16.					
17.					
18.					
19.					
20.					

So far, so good. You are building an inventory of the skills that you can offer to potential employers. The process doesn't add skills you don't have, it simply clarifies. As you go through the process, you are becoming more articulate about the things you can do. Along the way you can deviate from our rules if you wish and add additional criteria or skills whenever they occur. As you loosen up the resistance around expressing your abilities, you should get a strong flow of valuable information about yourself. Be sure to write it all down. You will use much of it in your resume.

• *Distillation* •

And now some sorting out. Review the twenty specific skills from Skill Summary Sheet One and check ten that combine the most value for others and satisfaction for you. List them below in order of importance to you and your worklife.

This inventory will be useful as you do further research into your job targets. Pay attention to the jargon or terminology commonly used in your field of interest to describe these skills. Think about the areas within the field where these skills are of most value.

Skill Summary Two

1. _____

2. _____

3. _____

4. _____

5. _____

6. _____

7. _____

8. _____

9. _____

10. _____

Block Two—Interests

When we talk about your interests in this process, we aren't just talking about curiosity. What we are looking for goes beyond mere curiosity and relaxed participation. We want more emotion in it. What are your turn-ons? What excites and challenges you? What would you walk a mile to do? *Those interests.*

And what would you like to know more about? What new games do you want to learn how to play? What about how to create a greater sense of aliveness, health, happiness, love, full self-expression? In the work formula, we want you to see these personal interests in addition to skills. Actually they are already very parallel subjects: people tend to excel in the things they enjoy.

When you locate jobs that work for you, you start to understand what "making it" is all about. And it's not hard to do this in today's active, generating, technodynamic work flow. Not at all. Even in times of tight employment, the breakthrough comes when you are willing to actually be responsible for managing the quality of your worklife and willing to have it your way. Interested? Continue following this process, and discover more.

• *Life and Work* •

Our mutual concern about interests in Block Two is not *directly* related to the resume you will produce. You don't feature interests on the resume—you feature the *value* you can provide to a prospective employer—the contribution you can make. However, you need to be conscious of your life interests so that the job targets you go after contain the underlying motive force that brings your life and your work together. Unfortunately, the stereotype from which most of us have obtained our beliefs about work is essentially this: *Work is what you do from nine to five, five days a week to maximize your earnings, and life starts after five and on weekends.*

Work is what you *have* to do to build your bank account, and "life" is what you *like* to do. This is the attitude that floats around high school corridors and college dormitories like the flu, and permeates even the highest career ranks. The prevailing ideal is to do as little as necessary, for as much as you can get.

Don't be trapped in this way of thinking. The only real struggle in work is put there by people who are not willing to be responsible for the quality of their life. Work and life happen at the same time. You are living 100 percent of the time when you are working and can bring to work the same personal scope you bring to your playtime. It boils down to a question of choice: When you are in touch with your essential interests and motivations and look out into the work world from this centered point of view, you begin to see work as *opportunity*—the opportunity to choose the skills you want to apply.

What does this have to do with your resume? Plenty. When you are in touch with your interests and turn-ons, as well as your skills and abilities, your resume becomes a passport to personal satisfaction rather than just a work permit.

• *The Pleasure Detector* •

Go down the list of the activities below and check off each one that could bring you a helping of personal pleasure. Don't stop to think when you read an item. If you get a small positive vibration, check it off even if you've never played the game before.

I like . . .

___ outdoor activities	___ fixing machines	___ raising money
___ giving advice	___ supervising others	___ interviewing people
___ theater	___ helping people	___ teaching
___ doing research	___ writing	___ taking care of children
___ persuading people	___ inventing	___ preparing a gourmet meal
___ singing or acting	___ computer games	___ making a good bargain
___ meeting new people	___ hacking	___ designing clothes
___ driving	___ jewelry making	___ collecting
___ collecting art	___ entertaining	___ navigating a sailboat
___ listening to music	___ working alone	___ solving problems
___ building things	___ taking risks	___ creating
___ repairing things	___ being my own boss	___ traveling
___ taking care of animals	___ routine, orderly tasks	___ exercising
___ designing and decorating	___ taking care of people	___ cabinetmaking
___ working physically	___ working with plants	___ antique hunting
___ working with numbers	___ counseling people	___ dressmaking
___ working with computers	___ reading	

How about your hobbies? Have they been covered? If not, write in here.

_____   _____

If you had a guaranteed income of $100,000 per year for life without working, what would you do with your time? If not covered above, write these activities here.

_____   _____

Secret pleasures? Let the hedonist in you out. List anything else below, even if you think it's slightly indulgent.

_____   _____

• *Pleasure Detector Synthesis* •

Now, synthesize. Go back over all of the items you came up with in the Pleasure Detector and boil them down to those you feel could bring the deepest personal satisfaction if you could blend them into your work.

Rank the ten personal interests you would most like to weave into your worklife or lifework.

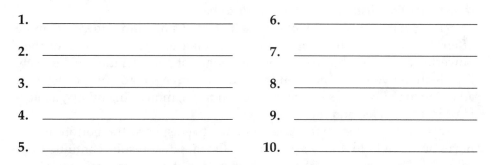

1. _____   6. _____

2. _____   7. _____

3. _____   8. _____

4. _____   9. _____

5. _____   10. _____

Block Three—Personal Qualities

Underneath your skills and interests there is still another you: that tenacious, irascible, courageous interface between the great world outside and the deep world inside, looking now one way and then the other in this adventure we call Life.

It is *you* they are hiring, not the stereotype that you might have confused yourself with. And we know that it *looks* as if they are interested in hiring the stereotype or work role. As a matter of fact, that's probably what they think, too. Actually, there is a stronger undercurrent at work.

Employers want to hire. Applicants forget that and often fall into an adversary, defensive posture. Organizations have one big underlying problem: to hire the right people to solve all of the other business problems and exploit the opportunities that define the purpose of the organization.

Employers know that what they need in the really important positions is not people to hammer all the pegs into holes or fill out endless reports, but *people who can get the job done.* They want people who start from a position of *mastery* and then learn to handle the details as they come along: problem solvers.

• *Leadership* •

Remember what we said earlier about what characterizes the work world of the '90s, the atmosphere or actionsphere of change. It encompasses increasing levels of technology, global markets, changing risks, sociological changes, lifestyle and workstyle changes. You must demonstrate those qualities you possess that will support the people you want to work for. Personal qualities are the generating principles that provide the power behind your work, sometimes called character.

Leadership qualities are important and, like all qualities (as opposed to skills), tend to be intangible, judgmental, and interpretive. For this reason they are harder to write about and need to be handled with care in resume language. (Often this intangible aspect has kept resume writers from including qualities at all—in many cases to their detriment.) The important thing is to use quality terms in connection with an accomplishment: "Worked with the product team to explore *innovative* new packaging approaches," rather than in a list: "I consider myself to be . . ."

Simply having good qualities doesn't create leadership. However, more often than not, it is the people who are willing to speak in terms of their powerful qualities who inspire others. Some of the qualities to honestly illuminate on your resume include: vision, courage, creativity, persistence, adapting to radical shifts in direction or condition, motivating others, achieving breakthroughs, and more.

Even with this new emphasis on qualitative aspects, the bottom line is never out of sight for today's employers. Quantitative results continue to be essential. The resume portraying a combination of good leadership qualities and powerful results—and showing constant improvement—is formidable.

If you plan to stress versatility and uniqueness, seriously consider the targeted and functional resume formats (see pp. 53, 54, 83, 91).

Given that computer power can be uniquely harnessed for resume production (see pp. 5, 71, 112), you might want several targeted variations on any given job target theme.

• Personal Qualities Profile •

1. Review the list of personal qualities below, focusing inward to the personal traits that you alone know best. Draw a line through all of the attributes that are *not* really you, that don't describe you. If you are on the fence about it, leave it in.

2. Go over the list again. This time circle each word that describes a quality clearly representing a facet of you.

3. In the space provided, write in any basic personal characteristics that aren't on our list but that you feel describe you at least as well.

Adaptable	Insightful	Versatile
Willing	Assertive	Perceptive
Thorough	Sensitive	Imaginative
Precise	Supportive	Creative
Caring	Productive	Efficient
Energetic	Trustworthy	Diligent
Honest	Communicative	Intelligent
Hard-working	Helpful	Intuitive
Courageous	Strong	Determined
Dedicated	Analytic	Committed

Forthright	Organized	Intellectual
Tenacious	Incisive	Persuasive
Responsible	Warm	Flexible
Persistent	Friendly	
	Humorous	

List any other qualities that apply to you.

_____

_____

_____

4. Select four of the personal qualities you circled—the most powerful four from your point of view—and list them in the space provided.

• *Primary Personal Qualities* •

FINAL SELECTION

1. _____

2. _____

3. _____

4. _____

Optional: Using the terms you have selected, write a two-paragraph description of yourself as it would appear in *Who's Who—Special Edition!*

Block Four: Results

Now it's time to shift gears. We have been operating for the previous several pages in an exploratory, introspective manner, looking at ways of communicating tangibly some qualities that are not always clearly evident to the outside world. We now want to turn the spotlight outward on your relationship with the physical universe—the world of results.

As used in this process, a result is a *tangible, measurable, final product, achievement, or accomplishment that you have produced or created out of your involvement or participation in a particular activity or job.* Results have a physical form. They are almost impossible to ignore. They are the precious stones in the setting of your resume. When you speak the language of results, people remember.

Compare these two statements:

- My duties included cost analysis, planning, work flow, scheduling construction activities, budgeting, and architectural design and engineering.

Or:

- I built the John Hancock Building in Boston.

Now close your eyes and see which one you can remember.

The more tangible results you have in your resume, the easier it is to get a strong and memorable picture of your capacity to do the job you seek.

Results come in all shapes and sizes and relate to every area of activity in your life. People frequently take what they do so much for granted that, when asked to describe what results they have produced, they have difficulty coming up with any. They look for something significant or award-winning and, falling short of that, they fail to mention anything.

We are going to ask you to inventory some of the results you have produced in your life, to list anything you can think of, large or small. Allow yourself to free associate—write down anything that comes to mind. You can edit it later.

• *Results Inventory* •

In each category shown on the following pages write down as many past results and achievements as you can think of. List whatever you think of even if you're not sure it fits that category, or even if you aren't sure that it's a result! Categories necessarily overlap. We have provided a few examples in each category to allow you to warm up to the idea.

SCHOOL AND OTHER TRAINING RESULTS

Think of achievements in other areas of training or know-how.

Our examples

- Wrote fifteen-page report and analysis of *Perestroika* by Mikhail Gorbachev
- Finished Katharine Gibbs steno course
- Completed AMA interviewing workshop
- Took Xerox sales-training program
- Developed fluency in French and Spanish
- Mastered wordprocessing and spreadsheets on IBM PC

Yours

_____

_____

_____

EXTRACURRICULAR RESULTS

Our examples

- Volunteered at a local recycling center
- Managed student blood drive—recruited twenty volunteers
- Edited class yearbook
- Raised over $1,000 for local election
- Earned over one hundred dollars per week in part-time work while carrying a full daytime class load
- Tutored students in Algebra and Trigonometry for statewide exams

List your results from school here:

_____

_____

_____

LEISURE-TIME RESULTS

List any results you have produced during vacation periods, weekends, after hours, other times off.

Our examples

- Managed state-champion Little League team
- Organized a wilderness trek for ten persons
- Designed costumes for three musicals at local summer tent theater
- Trained volunteers in Adult Literacy program
- Climbed Mount Washington
- Organized local political campaign

Yours

_____

_____

_____

HOBBY RESULTS

List any results or accomplishments you have achieved with any hobbies you have.

Our examples

- Read complete works of Isaac Bashevis Singer
- Built a digital synthesizer
- Earned scuba-diving certification
- Learned computer chess
- Served as auctioneer for P.T.A. annual auction

Yours

_____

_____

_____

MILITARY RESULTS

If you have had any military experience, look creatively at what the results were for you.

Our examples

- Mastered military occupational specialty in photojournalism
- Completed command and general staff college
- Served as supply clerk, organized system
- Supervised a detachment of twelve service members and civilian employees
- Learned the German language

Yours

_____

_____

_____

COMMUNITY RESULTS

Where have you participated in community affairs and achieved something of value? Include volunteer and paid work.

Our examples

- Helped set up counseling program for aged
- Managed weekend recycling center
- Organized opposition to chemical plant location
- Supervised Meals on Wheels program

Yours

_____

_____

_____

HOME RESULTS

Don't ignore the obvious achievements that you have been responsible for at home, particularly if you haven't had much paid work experience.

Our examples

- Helped remodel an old ten-room house
- Managed small family trust fund
- Repaired home appliances
- Prepared family tax returns
- Managed family budget

Yours

_____

_____

_____

MISCELLANEOUS RESULTS

List any achievements, final products, results, or solutions to problems that you haven't written down yet, and that you feel demonstrate your capabilities.

_____

_____

Your most recent work experience

Position _____ Dates _____

Employer _____

List five accomplishments or results produced:

_____

_____

_____

_____

_____

Earlier work experience

Position _____ Dates _____

Employer _____

List five accomplishments or results produced:

_____

_____

_____

_____

_____

Earlier work experience

Position _____ Dates _____

Employer _____

List five accomplishments or results produced:

_____

_____

_____

_____

_____

Go back and read over all of the work-related or nonwork results you have listed from page 33 to page 36, selecting the ones you consider most relevant to your possible future work and grading them with check marks as follows:

√   not relevant to my future work
√√   somewhat relevant to my future work
√√√   quite relevant to my future work

Be careful not to rate any item low in relevance simply because it may have occurred in a different field of work. If the way you accomplished the result could be relevant to your next work assignment, that will qualify it.

From the ones you have checked, select the ten past results that in your view are *most relevant to your future work.*

1. _____
2. _____
3. _____
4. _____
5. _____

6. _____
7. _____
8. _____
9. _____
10. _____

Congratulations!

If you have completed the preceding analysis of four resume building blocks, you have done more in preparation for your resume than at least 95 percent of your colleagues and competitors in the job market. You have made a major contribution to yourself and your work consciousness, and the results in your resume and job campaign will show it.

Possibly, you ran into some confusion or personal barriers along the way as you put the searchlight on yourself. This is not an easy process, and many people have difficulty with self-appraisal. Shortly we're going to show you how to summarize the information. Before you do that, however, if you feel you could improve what you've already done, go back over the lists again and add to them. Remember, it's *your* perfect resume we're after.

Summarizing the Four Blocks

You have now completed the basic components of your resume. (Work history, education, and personal data will be next.) Summarize below what you've captured so far.

• Block One: Skills •

(You can pick these up from Skill Summary Two, page 26.)

1. _____   6. _____

2. _____   7. _____

3. _____   8. _____

4. _____   9. _____

5. _____   10. _____

• Block Two: Interests •

(You can pick these up from Pleasure Detector Synthesis, page 29.)

1. _____   6. _____

2. _____   7. _____

3. _____   8. _____

4. _____   9. _____

5. _____   10. _____

• Block Three: Personal Qualities •

(You can pick these up from Primary Personal Qualities, page 31.)

1. _____

2. _____

3. _____

4. _____

• Block Four: Results •

All of the above have combined to create the following major achievements and results in your life.
(You can pick these up from The Top Ten, page 37.)

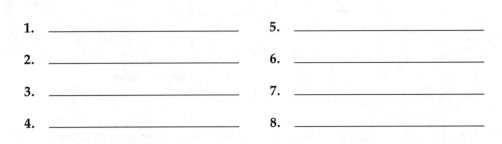

1. _____	5. _____
2. _____	6. _____
3. _____	7. _____
4. _____	8. _____

You now have the basic building blocks that will allow you to focus on job targets and a perfect resume to get you just what you want in the work world. This puts you in the top 10 percent of your career competitors. . . . Be proud!

JOB TARGETING

If you are very clear about your personal job targets, you can skip this part, and move directly to page 49.

Imagine for a moment that you are an employer. Say, for example, that you are the manager of customer service for a small software firm. It is your job to ensure that any complaints or service requirements from purchasers of your programs are satisfied promptly, professionally, and in a way that encourages customer loyalty.

As manager, you have six service representatives who are in communication with customers, primarily by phone, to a lesser degree by letter, and occasionally in person. One of your service reps is leaving, and you are screening candidates for his/her replacement. With your job requirement in mind, and knowing that you have a large pile of resumes to get through, read the two resume paragraphs on p. 40.

Yes—you guessed it—another before-and-after story. The same person with two different approaches to the same experience. In the second example the unnecessary details have been eliminated, and the switch made from chronological and "duty" oriented to a more targeted functional approach focusing on "results" in the sales and service aspects of a customer service job target.

Advantage: Greatly enhanced attention by the employer, and a probable interview.

By targeting his/her resume, our candidate made it easy for the employer to notice the points of his/her experience that would be related to the employer's needs.

Like a good advertisement, the resume works best when the writer has a clear idea of who the "prospect" is and what that person wants. It's that basic.

1986—Present—Sales Trainee—Photo Ion, Inc.
                              633 La Cienega Drive
                              Los Angeles, California

As one of seven persons in the Sales department I was responsible for
dealing with customers on a variety of levels, in introducing the Mark IV
electronic photocopier in the Western five-state region (California,
Nevada, Oregon, Washington, Colorado). My duties included screening new
prospects, setting up meetings, assisting in sales calls, helping with
installations and responding to customer complaints.

Customer Service Experience

* Assisted in introduction of new electronic projects to customers in
  Western states.
* Worked with over fifty companies to increase acceptance and use of
  innovative copying system.
* Helped to reduce customer complaints by 50% in 90 days.
* Mastered complex equipment servicing in record time.

THE UNIVERSAL HIRING RULE

**Any employer will hire any individual as long as the employer is convinced
that the hiring will bring more value than its cost.**

   As we have said, contrary to popular opinion employers are very interested in hiring. That's their job: to locate the best people and equipment to
get the work done. This is true in employment downturns as well as periods
of high demand. Employers always need people who can produce results:
profits, safety, cost-cutting, organization, innovative solutions. These words (and
deeds) are music to the ears of any manager or supervisor who is under
pressure to upgrade results in her/his department.

The disturbing difficulty from the vantage of guidance and career counselors is that most job candidates don't seem to understand the rules. Left to their own devices, the average job seekers, more times than not, will virtually obscure the major sales points in their resumes with too much additional information, unclear writing style, and lack of direction.

Targeting your resume means to aim its thrust directly at the most obvious needs of a particular employment opportunity or job target. If you don't know the kind of work or company you want to hitch up with, the resume becomes too general to really strike the heart of the right employer. Even though most of the information is from the past, when you know what you're going for, and do a little research, you can demonstrate future potential in the targeted employer's own language.

Your Job Target

A job target is a particular work description or title in a given field. It is not a specific job opening, but rather a title that could exist with a number of employers. For example: *service rep, cost accountant, travel agent, wellness director* are all job targets. Your resume will be dramatically more valuable and communicative if it has been fashioned for a job target that you have worked out in advance. Once you are clear about the target, it becomes obvious what to include and what to leave out.

Given the enormous diversity of opportunity in today's work environment, you will probably have two or three job targets in related or, in some cases, different fields reflecting diverse sets of interests and skills. In completing part one of the Career Discovery Process you have unearthed much of what is needed to construct your job targets.

Our basic requirement for your job target is that it *starts with you*. You put it together using your skills and interests. If you target job areas relating only to your skills, your work will miss that essential pleasure bond that keeps the juices of motivation and satisfaction flowing. On the other hand, if you go after areas of interest where there isn't a viable skill base, you won't have much to describe in your resume or interview.

A job target is something that you are aiming for. It lies along a course line, or lifeline, and can include a short-term job goal as well as a long-term career direction. For example, your three-year target could be as an employment manager and your immediate job goal might be as an interviewer or recruiter.

With clear job targets you are in charge of your work search, and your resume reflects this clarity. Without a job target, your approach to the employment market is mostly opportunistic and will involve many false starts, wrong turns, and dead ends. The extra work involved in targeting pays dividends in the ease of organizing your job search and resume, and of course the big payoff is that you end up doing work that reflects who you are and brings you increased day-to-day satisfaction.

• Job Target List •

If you are already very clear about one or more job targets for yourself, list them here:

My first job target is:_____

My second job target is:_____

My third job target is:_____

If these targets are completely satisfying for you, move directly to page 49.

Job Target Creation

If you haven't pulled together your job targets yet, here is a short process that will help. Follow these instructions:

1. Go back to your list of specific skills on page 38 and select five major skills. List them below.
2. Also, list your five major interests from page 38.

• Five Major Skills •	*• Five Major Interests •*
_____	_____
_____	_____
_____	_____
_____	_____
_____	_____

3. Next, mix and match these skills and interests in some exploratory steps, which require you to give up any preconceived ideas about your job title and uncover alternatives you might not have considered.

In the spaces below list pairs of skills and interests and then come up with job titles you feel combine these. Pick skills and interests you feel could be tied together in a variety of job possibilities. Don't limit yourself only to combinations that reflect what you've already decided about yourself. And in coming up with the job titles, be willing to stretch your imagination a bit—list titles that may not be directly relevant to your idea of what you want to do. Play around!

Here are some examples of what we mean:

The skill of _negotiating_
and
The interest in _working with people_

could combine in the following job possibilities:
1. _Industrial Relations Manager_
2. _Arbitrator_
3. _Marriage counselor_

The skill of _purchasing/buying_
and
The interest in _business systems_

could combine in the following job possibilities:
1. _Software consultant_
2. _Project Manager_
3. _Systems planner_

The skill of _communication_
and
The interest in _travel_

could combine in the following job possibilities:
1. _Public Relations specialist_
2. _International trainer_
3. _Convention planner_

The skill of _word processing_
and
The interest in _dancing_

could combine in the following job possibilities:
1. _Administrator for theater_
2. _Fundraiser for ballet company_
3. _Assistant editor - dance magazine_

It's your turn: In the spaces below, write down skills and interests from your lists in combinations that could relate to work situations. You may use the same interests and skills more than once. (If you get stuck and need more, you may go back to your original skills and interests lists on pages 26 and 29.) Don't stop until you have at least *twenty* job possibilities in the right-hand margin. Write things down even if your mind raises the red flags of "I can't" or "I won't."

The skill of _____
and
The interest in _____

could combine in the following job possibilities:
1. _____
2. _____
3. _____

The skill of _____ could combine in the following job
    and possibilities:
The interest in _____ 1. _____
    2. _____
    3. _____

The skill of _____ could combine in the following job
    and possibilities:
The interest in _____ 1. _____
    2. _____
    3. _____

The skill of _____ could combine in the following job
    and possibilities:
The interest in _____ 1. _____
    2. _____
    3. _____

The skill of _____ could combine in the following job
    and possibilities:
The interest in _____ 1. _____
    2. _____
    3. _____

The skill of _____ could combine in the following job
    and possibilities:
The interest in _____ 1. _____
    2. _____
    3. _____

The skill of _____ could combine in the following job
    and possibilities:
The interest in _____ 1. _____
    2. _____
    3. _____

The skill of _____ could combine in the following job
    and possibilities:
The interest in _____ 1. _____
    2. _____
    3. _____

The skill of _____   could combine in the following job
       and   possibilities:
The interest in _____   **1.** _____
        2. _____
        3. _____

The skill of _____   could combine in the following job
       and   possibilities:
The interest in _____   **1.** _____
        2. _____
        3. _____

• *Selected Job Titles* •

If you had difficulty coming up with job titles to match your skills and
interests, don't be alarmed, for many people have the same problem. The
mind sometimes goes blank when confronted by the immensity of the work
world.

To stimulate your thinking, here is a list of well over 200 job titles selected
from employment classified advertisements around the country. Read through
them, expanding your mind. If you get some new ideas from this list, add
them to the job targets you came up with previously.

Software designer
Foundation director
Lyricist
Speech therapist
Air traffic controller
Quality assurance
    analyst
Project leader
Insurance agent
X-ray technician
Plan administrator
Occupational
    therapist
Meteorologist
Paramedic
Product manager
Auditor

Furniture maker
Composer
Collector
Database administrator
Packaging expert
Child care worker
Geographer
Physicist
Statistician
PR medial specialist
Music coordinator
Marketeer
EEC marketing consultant
Sound engineer
Physical therapist
Reporter
Politician

Social director
Research assistant
Hotel manager
Urban planning director
Broker
Comptroller
Actuary
Dietitian
Travel agent
Novelist
Social worker
Musician
Account executive
Literary critic
Dancer
Circulation manager
Machinist

Veterinarian
Translator
Equities trader
Entomologist
Sales representative
Marketing
  coordinator
Industrial relations
  manager
Actor/actress
Environmental
  analyst
Chemical process
  engineer
College recruiter
Accounting clerk
Interior designer
Scuba instructor
Community relations
  director
Computer operator
Budget manager
Buyer
Debt administrator
Labor relations
  specialist
Underwriter
Securities attorney
Restaurant manager
LAN administrator
Illustrator
Linguist
EDP auditor
Programmer
Word processor
Office manager
Investment banker
Copywriter
Lecturer
Zoologist
Benefits
  administrator
Risk manager
Political aide
Geologist
Navigator

Agriculturist
Designer
Economist
Consumer advocate
Tax specialist
Retail closeout buyer
Real estate analyst
Nurse
Fashion model
Architect
Estimator
Botanist
Photographer
Cable TV producer
Traffic manager
Career counselor
Market researcher
Caseworker
Nutritionist
Management consultant
Set designer
Trade show manager
Carpenter
Financial analyst
Physician
International sales
  engineer
Window display artist
Management trainee
Image consultant
Video catalogue producer
Environmental control
  manager
Toxic waste consultant
Director of telemarketing
Stress control therapist
Robotics engineer
Space scientist
Accountant
Credit manager
Graphic designer
Stockbroker
Toy designer
Program analyst
Receptionist
Fund raiser

Compensation specialist
Mechanic
Systems analyst
Telecommunication
  specialist
International bond
  salesperson
Solid state circuit
  designer
Word processing
  coordinator
Videotext specialist
Leveraged buyout dealer
Financial systems
  specialist
Artificial intelligence
  designer
Disarmament negotiator
Resume consultant
Micromedical technician
TV producer
Oceanographer
Media planner
Tax manager
Administrative assistant
Civil engineer
Inspector
Journalist
Lab technician
College professor
Career developer
Survey sampling
  statistician
Instructor
Landscape designer
Special projects manager
Human resources
  specialist
Mortgage securities
  researcher
Executive
Writer
Tennis pro
Geneticist
R & D manager
Exporter

Negotiator
Audiologist
Editor
Caterer
Food scientist
Photo journalist
Media analyst
Nautilus trainer
Psychologist

Bookkeeper
Anthropologist
Customer service
    representative
Systems development
    analyst
Chef
Medical technologist
Publisher

Chemist
Reference librarian
Biologist
Merchandise controller
Analyst
Attorney
Legislator
Printer
Teacher

4. Narrow down.

The idea now is to take your expanded exploratory job possibility lists. Select ten to twelve possibilities from pages 45 to 47 and narrow them down to something real. Go back over the list and transcribe each to the appropriate column below, indicating your current thinking as to how much satisfaction this title could provide you if it were yours.

Very Satisfying	*Somewhat Satisfying*	*Not Satisfying*
_____	_____	_____
_____	_____	_____
_____	_____	_____
_____	_____	_____
_____	_____	_____
_____	_____	_____
_____	_____	_____
_____	_____	_____
_____	_____	_____
_____	_____	_____

Then rank-number the titles in each column in accordance with how "practical" you feel this title would be as a real job target for you. You can use any meaning you wish to define this practically for yourself.

5. Bottom line.

If all went well, and you pushed through the complexities of this targeting process, you have handled four very important variables that underlie your perfect resume: *skill, interest, satisfaction, and practicality.*

You should know that by following this job-targeting process you have already put more consciousness into your work campaign than most of the population. You have gotten closer to job targets that represent the essential you and that can produce the satisfaction and aliveness that make work truly satisfying.

Finally, reduce your list to three or four targets you would be willing to go after with energy, and in the pursuit of which you would be *willing* to prepare a perfect resume. You may make this final selection by using any criteria you wish. We've taken you this far—you make the final choice on your terms and list your choices below.

MY JOB TARGETS ARE:

First job target _____

Second job target _____

Third job target _____

Now review your choices and see if you are satisfied with the decisions you have made. If not, track backward through the process and modify any choices you made. When you are confident about your selections, acknowledge yourself and move along to the next part of the perfect resume process.

Preparing Your Perfect Resume

YOU BE THE JUDGE—

Shown below is an actual resume from a person who wrote it without any clarity about his job target. Pretend to be an employer and read it with a view toward understanding how the person could assist you.

On the next page is a revised version of the same person's resume.

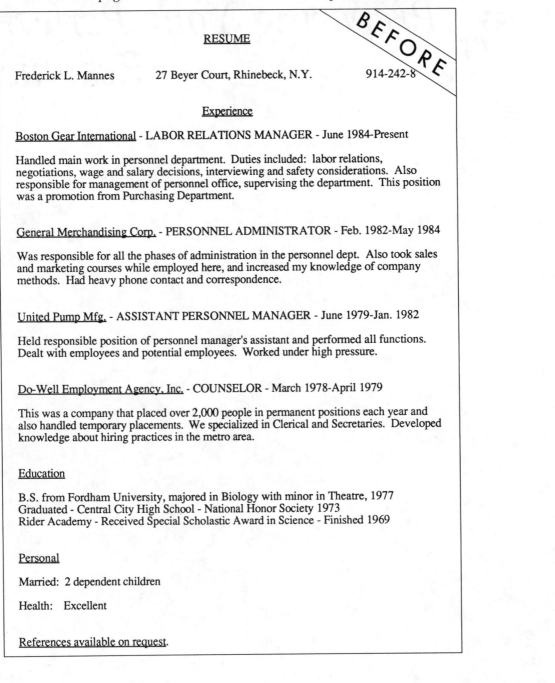

RESUME

BEFORE

Frederick L. Mannes   27 Beyer Court, Rhinebeck, N.Y.   914-242-8

Experience

Boston Gear International - LABOR RELATIONS MANAGER - June 1984-Present

Handled main work in personnel department. Duties included: labor relations, negotiations, wage and salary decisions, interviewing and safety considerations. Also responsible for management of personnel office, supervising the department. This position was a promotion from Purchasing Department.

General Merchandising Corp. - PERSONNEL ADMINISTRATOR - Feb. 1982-May 1984

Was responsible for all the phases of administration in the personnel dept. Also took sales and marketing courses while employed here, and increased my knowledge of company methods. Had heavy phone contact and correspondence.

United Pump Mfg. - ASSISTANT PERSONNEL MANAGER - June 1979-Jan. 1982

Held responsible position of personnel manager's assistant and performed all functions. Dealt with employees and potential employees. Worked under high pressure.

Do-Well Employment Agency, Inc. - COUNSELOR - March 1978-April 1979

This was a company that placed over 2,000 people in permanent positions each year and also handled temporary placements. We specialized in Clerical and Secretaries. Developed knowledge about hiring practices in the metro area.

Education

B.S. from Fordham University, majored in Biology with minor in Theatre, 1977
Graduated - Central City High School - National Honor Society 1973
Rider Academy - Received Special Scholastic Award in Science - Finished 1969

Personal

Married: 2 dependent children

Health: Excellent

References available on request.

YOU BE THE JUDGE—

Here is the resume the same person wrote after becoming clear about his primary job target and using some of the procedures in this book. (Incidentally, he also prepared a different resume for his secondary job target as college recruiter.)

FREDERICK L. MANNES
27 Beyer Court
Rhinebeck, New York 11293
(914) 242-8874

AFTER

JOB TARGET: **EMPLOYEE BENEFITS EXECUTIVE**

ABILITIES:
- Direct a comprehensive employee benefits program for over 30,000 employees.
- Negotiate contracts with insurance and other benefits personnel.
- Manage labor relations negotiations and pre-negotiating planning.
- Analyze health-care programs for cost-effectiveness.
- Research both salaried and hourly benefits programs.
- Closely monitor federal, state, and local legislation and identify potential labor problems.
- Accurately and clearly communicate details of benefits programs to both employer and employees.

ACHIEVEMENTS:
- Developed employee benefits programs for over 250 hourly employees.
- Negotiated benefits contracts resulting in 17% savings on premiums.
- Identified potential problems in new legislation, thus avoiding several potentially costly lawsuits.
- Directed research on major new medical benefits program.
- Set cost-control standards which have since been adopted throughout pump industry.
- Developed new kit for use in communicating benefits program to hourly employees.

WORK HISTORY:

1984 - Present	BOSTON GEAR INTERNATIONAL Labor Relations Manager	White Plains, NY
1982 - 1984	GENERAL MERCHANDISING CORP. Personnel Administrator	Stamford, CT
1979 - 1982	UNITED PUMP MANUFACTURING Assistant Personnel Manager	Stamford, CT
1978 - 1979	Employment Counselor	

EDUCATION:

| 1979 | FORDHAM UNIVERSITY - New York, NY
B.A. Degree | |

STEP 1: SELECTING A RESUME FORMAT

Now that you have discovered, or rediscovered, or affirmed (or just settled for) your job targets and have completed—or bypassed—the Career Discovery Process, you are ready to put your resume together and start to handle the important technical details of its preparation. The steps are simple and the instructions clear, so go to it and have fun. The work you are doing will pay off handsomely in the final product.

In the best modern architectural and design studios you will frequently hear the expression *form follows function* bandied about. Manufacturing and organizational experts use it too. The contemporary approach is to create structures that efficiently accomplish their purpose without unnecessary ornamentation or outdated stereotypes.

The same principle applies to your resume. For best results you should use a form or format that reflects the particular demands or requirements of your own job targets and work history.

If you haven't had much experience with resumes, it might surprise you to learn that there are at least five possible formats for your resume. If you've had a lot of experience with reviewing resumes, the surprise might be that we refer to *only* five, since from an employer's point of view it seems that the varieties are endless—sometimes hopeless!

In fact, although there are many different *layouts*, there are really only five basic resume formats that you need to know. These are:

Chronological Format

Work experience and personal history arranged in reverse time sequence.

Functional Format

Work experience and abilities cataloged by major areas of involvement—sometimes with dates, sometimes without.

Targeted Format

A highly future-focused presentation directed to a very specific job target.

Resume Alternative

A special purpose communication for people for whom a resume isn't appropriate due to lack of experience.

Creative Alternative

A free form approach for artsy-craftsy folk.

CHRONOLOGICAL RESUME

JACK DEUTSCH
415 Sommer Road
Warwick, NY 10990
(914) 968-6357

WORK EXPERIENCE:

1985 - Present   FINES APPAREL, INC.   New York, NY

Divisional Controller

Report directly to the Chief Financial Officer. Manage cash funds. Prepare consolidated corporate tax returns for seven companies and financial review of major subsidiaries. Design and prepare a monthly sales comparison report for corporate executives. Co-supervisor of accounting for a $150-million company.

1984 - 1985   STACEY'S, INC.   New York, NY

Corporate Auditor

Reported directly to the Assistant Corporate Controller. Conducted operational and financial audits within the Treasurer's office and five operating divisions. Developed a report with findings and recommendations for the CEO of each division and numerous management personnel.

1977 - 1984   PRICE, WETHERAU & COMPANY   New York, NY

Supervising Senior

Joined the professional staff as an assistant accountant. Reported directly to partners and managers. Planned, supervised, and completed numerous audit assignments.

AWARDS / ACCREDITATIONS / MEMBERSHIPS:

1981   Certified Public Accountant, New York State

1977   American Institute of Certified Public Accountants
New York State Society of Certified Public Accountants

EDUCATION:

1977   HOFSTRA UNIVERSITY
B.S. in Accounting

FUNCTIONAL RESUME

MARILYN M. GUNTER
792 Cliff Court
Portland, OR 97208
(503) 249-8862

INSURANCE LAW:

• Advised management of insurance company on legality of insurance transactions.
• Studied court decisions and recommended changes in wording of insurance policies to conform with law and/or to protect company from unwarranted claims.
• Advised claims department personnel of legality of claims filed on company to insure against undue payments.
• Advised personnel engaged in drawing up of legal documents such as insurance contracts and release papers.

CORPORATE LAW:

• Extensively studied corporation structure, including legal rights, obligations and privileges.
• Acted as agent for several corporations in various transactions.
• Studied decisions, statutes, and ordinances of quasi-judicial bodies.

REAL ESTATE LAW:

• Handled sale and transfer of real property.
• Instituted title searches to establish ownership.
• Drew up deeds, mortgages, and leases.
• Acted as trustee of property and held funds for investment.

WORK EXPERIENCE:

1980 - Present   COMMERCIAL AUTOMOBILE UNDERWRITERS COMPANY, INC.
Portland, OR

Insurance Services Office Supervisor

EDUCATION:

1987   UNIVERSITY OF OREGON LAW SCHOOL
LLB - Insurance Law, Corporate Law, Estate Planning, Income Taxation

1980   UNIVERSITY OF OREGON
B.A. Degree; History Major

RESUME FORMATS

Chronological

Notice that in this resume the job history is shown from the most recent job backward—with the most recent job having the most space. Titles and organizations are emphasized and duties and accomplishments within those titles described.

Advantages: emphasizes continuity and career growth. Highlights name of employer. Easy to follow.

Best used: when your career direction is clear and the job target is directly in line with your work history, or the name of your last employer adds strong prestige.

Functional

This format highlights major areas of accomplishment and strength and allows you to organize them in an order that most supports your work objectives and job targets. Actual titles and work history are in a subordinate position and sometimes left off entirely.

Advantages: gives you considerable flexibility in emphasis. Eliminates repetition of job assignments. Tends to de-emphasize experience.

Best used: in cases of career change or redirection, first-job search, or reentry into the job market. Effective when you wish to play up a particularly strong area of ability.

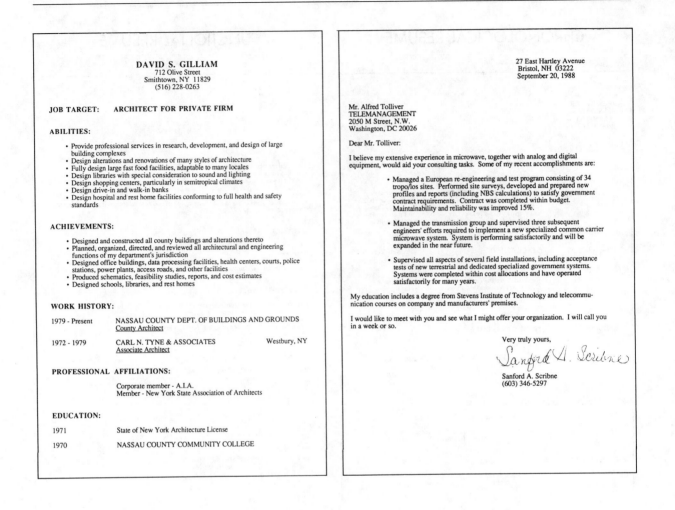

DAVID S. GILLIAM
712 Olive Street
Smithtown, NY 11829
(516) 228-0263

JOB TARGET: ARCHITECT FOR PRIVATE FIRM

ABILITIES:

- Provide professional services in research, development, and design of large building complexes
- Design alterations and renovations of many styles of architecture
- Fully design large fast food facilities, adaptable to many locales
- Design libraries with special consideration to sound and lighting
- Design shopping centers, particularly in semitropical climates
- Design drive-in and walk-in banks
- Design hospital and rest home facilities conforming to full health and safety standards

ACHIEVEMENTS:

- Designed and constructed all county buildings and alterations thereto
- Planned, organized, directed, and reviewed all architectural and engineering functions of my department's jurisdiction
- Designed office buildings, data processing facilities, health centers, courts, police stations, power plants, access roads, and other facilities
- Produced schematics, feasibility studies, reports, and cost estimates
- Designed schools, libraries, and rest homes

WORK HISTORY:

1979 - Present   NASSAU COUNTY DEPT. OF BUILDINGS AND GROUNDS
                   County Architect

1972 - 1979   CARL N. TYNE & ASSOCIATES   Westbury, NY
                   Associate Architect

PROFESSIONAL AFFILIATIONS:

                   Corporate member - A.I.A.
                   Member - New York State Association of Architects

EDUCATION:

1971   State of New York Architecture License

1970   NASSAU COUNTY COMMUNITY COLLEGE

---

27 East Hartley Avenue
Bristol, NH 03222
September 20, 1988

Mr. Alfred Tolliver
TELEMANAGEMENT
2050 M Street, N.W.
Washington, DC 20026

Dear Mr. Tolliver:

I believe my extensive experience in microwave, together with analog and digital equipment, would aid your consulting tasks. Some of my recent accomplishments are:

- Managed a European re-engineering and test program consisting of 34 tropo/los sites. Performed site surveys, developed and prepared new profiles and reports (including NBS calculations) to satisfy government contract requirements. Contract was completed within budget. Maintainability and reliability was improved 15%.

- Managed the transmission group and supervised three subsequent engineers' efforts required to implement a new specialized common carrier microwave system. System is performing satisfactorily and will be expanded in the near future.

- Supervised all aspects of several field installations, including acceptance tests of new terrestrial and dedicated specialized government systems. Systems were completed within cost allocations and have operated satisfactorily for many years.

My education includes a degree from Stevens Institute of Technology and telecommunication courses on company and manufacturers' premises.

I would like to meet with you and see what I might offer your organization. I will call you in a week or so.

Very truly yours,

Sanford A. Scribne
(603) 346-5297

Targeted

This format is best for focusing on a clear, specific job target (you would have a different one for each target). It lists future-related capabilities and supporting accomplishments that relate to a clear job target.

Advantages: it makes a very impressive case for the one selected job, at the expense of other areas. It demonstrates a strong understanding and ability in the targeted area. It is future-directed.

Best used: when you are clear about your job targets and what they require.

Resume Alternative

This is a personal letter to a particular employer, addressing specific areas where you can be of value to that employer. It *demonstrates* your abilities as much as it describes them. It provides enough factual information to avoid the need for a resume, hopefully.

Advantages: creates employer interest without requiring a full resume. Addresses particular researched needs.

Best used: by people who have little or no work experience or background who are willing to do the required research for each letter.

Creative Alternative

Not for everyone, the creative resume tosses customary forms to the winds and demonstrates a highly polished individual approach. It should be used only in areas where this kind of creativity is related to the job target. Unless extremely well done, this approach can flop miserably. When done with great skill, it works very well.

Advantages: it gets read and frequently circulated to others. Makes one or two main points very clearly. Form can be varied indefinitely.

Best used: by writers; artists; and theatrical design, public relations, and media persons.

SELECTION PROCESS

Listed below are summaries of advantages and disadvantages of each type of resume we have covered. Check each statement that applies to you on all five formats, then select the format best for you. If you are still unclear about which format to choose, try doing a couple of approaches and comparing the results when you get to Step 2.

Chronological _____

IS advantageous
  * when name of last employer is an important consideration.
  * when staying in same field as prior jobs.
  * when job history shows real growth and development.
  * when prior titles are impressive.
  * in highly traditional fields (education, government).

is NOT advantageous
  * when work history is spotty.
  * when changing career goals.
  * when you have changed employers too frequently.
  * when you wish to deemphasize age.
  * when you have been doing the same thing too long.
  * when you have been absent from the job market for a while.
  * when you are looking for your first job.

Functional _____

IS advantageous
  * when you want to emphasize capabilities not used in recent work experience.
  * when changing careers.

- when entering job market for first time.
- when reentering job market after an absence.
- if career growth in past has not been good.
- when you have had a variety of different, relatively unconnected work experiences.
- where much of your work has been free-lance, consulting, or temporary.

is NOT advantageous
- when you want to emphasize a management growth pattern.
- for highly traditional fields such as teaching, ministerial, political, where the specific employers are of paramount interest.
- where you have performed a limited number of functions in your work.
- when your most recent employers have been *highly* prestigious.

Targeted

Includes most of the advantages and disadvantages of the functional resume and these further considerations:

IS advantageous
- when you are very clear about your job target.
- when you have several directions to go and want a different resume for each.
- when you want to emphasize capabilities you possess, but for which you may not have *paid* experience.

is NOT advantageous
- when you want to use one resume for several applications.
- when you are not clear about your capabilities and accomplishments.
- when you are just starting your career and have little experience.

Resume Alternative

IS advantageous
- when you have had little or no work experience.
- when you have been out of the job market for a long time.
- when you are willing to do solid research on a particular *employer* of interest.
- when you know or can find out the name of the person who will make the hiring decision.

is NOT advantageous
- when you have had enough experience to warrant a functional or chronological resume.
- if you have not decided what you want to do.
- if you are not clear about the contribution you can make to an organization.

Creative Alternative

IS advantageous
- in fields in which written or visual creativity are prime requisites of the job.
- when the medium of your work is appropriate to a printed form.

is NOT advantageous
- if you are planning to go through personnel.
- if you are not very sure of your creative ability.
- if you are looking for a management position.

It's your move. After having reviewed the five resume formats and checked all of the appropriate statements for advantages and disadvantages, which format do you wish to follow? (Note: It's possible to do more than one.) Check below the resume format you feel will best represent you.

_____ Chronological Resume	_____ Resume Alternative
_____ Functional Resume	_____ Creative Alternative
_____ Targeted Resume	

STEP 2: POWER PARAGRAPHS

Now the pace quickens, as you move from the introspective and elusive definitions of your essential qualities and work purposes into the more tangible task of actually writing your resume. Your investment in self-analysis will pay off in more clarity and direction in your resume and in your overall job search.

To this point you have chosen two or three job targets and a format that would best communicate your accomplishments and skills. Now in Step 2 you will learn the basic writing rules that apply to your resume. In Step 3 you will write the first draft of your own perfect resume.

AN ADVERTISEMENT FOR YOURSELF

The perfect resume is not a biography or memoir. It is not a detailed history of your life and times. Perhaps, surprisingly, it is not even an application for employment. A perfect resume is a well-structured, easy-to-read presentation of your capabilities and accomplishments, designed to convince a potential employer to invite you for an interview. A self-advertisement.

Designed to convince? Is it aggressive, bragging, immodest? No, not at all. We are continually surprised to run into students, workers, and even career counselors who take the position that job seekers should *underplay* their enthusiasm, avoid direct statements of personal ability. They suggest substituting the reluctant "I would like to try" for the imperative "I can!" Bad advice. If you doubt this, ask how does the organization you are applying to describe *its* services or products? Do they hide their strengths? Play down their capabilities? Obscure their primary accomplishments? If so, we're willing to have you take the soft line. But, frankly, we don't know many of these. On the contrary, we find that the most productive and exciting organizations have very little hesitancy to let you know who they are and what they can do.

We're not talking about *hype* or inflated self-praise or lies. We are talking about a clear, unembarrassed portrayal of yourself, presented in the best possible light. Show the picture of you with all systems go, and all the stops out. You know who we mean—that side of you that wakes up to the challenge, that surprises your friends and family. That's the person we want you to write about. Leave out the parts about warts and pimples, the times when you turned the wrong corner and forgot to set the alarm.

JOB ATTRACTORS

Here are some of the job attractors, power words, and phrases to favor in this turbulent decade:

- your ability to move seamlessly, swiftly, and capably from task to task, one work environment to another, soft product to hard product, and—for high flyers—across national boundaries.
- your ability to master new concepts, ideas, and practices.
- versatility, flexibility, mobility.
- high learning curve, adaptive to change, engaging problems innovatively.
- organizing and reorganizing new data, work systems, and corporate processes. Working integratively.
- entrepreneurial, and risk-smart.
- customer focused.
- cross-cultural, diversity.
- computer literate.
- multi-networked, information-related.
- work on special task forces, project teams.
- EEC and other internationalisms.
- thinking globally and acting locally.
- quality orientation.

Since the currency of today's job market is multinational, emphasize second and third languages—whether they be human communication or data-base communication.

THE ONE-PAGE RULE

A famous speaker once said that, if you are willing to stay with the major points, you can tell your whole life story in two minutes, and still have time left over for questions. You may not yet be at that level of communication, but without question, regardless of your experience or education, you can present everything you need to say in your resume in one page.

Yes, one page—even though you have had six jobs and three multimedia degrees. In over a dozen years of reading and correcting resumes in the uncounted thousands, we have not yet found one that didn't work better on one page. As most great writers, architects, and advertising agencies know, *less is more*.

After you eliminate repetitions, reinforcements, and redundancies, what's left communicates. Anyone who has had to read stacks of incoming mail will recognize the satisfaction and clarity of a short letter that makes its point, compared with the resistance to a two- or three-page document. The shorter presentation emphasizes the important information.

Although not scientifically documented, most personnel people agree that a two-page resume reduces readability and retention by 25 to 30 percent. As for a three-page resume, forget it. Readership is down by nearly half. An axiom of most resume experts is that very frequently the poorer, less-confident candidates have the longest resumes.

Exception to the One-Page Rule

If you have written a variety of articles or books, received an impressive list of honors or awards, obtained a dozen or so patents, or worked on a number of recognizable products, and the details of this list would encourage an employer to see you, then you might want to consider an *addendum* to your resume—a separate listing of these specific items. The important thing is to make it clear that your resume *ends* on the first page. The addendum is a list of examples rather than part of the page-one story.

At the bottom of the first sheet add something like "list of publications attached," so it's clear that, if the recruiter wishes, he can get the full story without turning the page.

Paring the Excess Fat from Your Resume

1. **Shorten sentences.** Eliminate long windups and connections. For example, the sentence "I was the person chosen to coordinate the college fund-raising team for the homecoming week" can be restated as "Coordinated college fund-raising team."

2. **Eliminate repetitions.** If you did similar tasks in two or three different jobs, explain in detail only in your most recent position.

3. Don't spell out information that is already implied or included in other information. If you are a college graduate, there is no reason to describe your high school education.

4. Leave off company addresses or names of references (you can provide them at the interview if requested). You don't even have to state "references provided on request." This is assumed.

5. List only most recent positions. If you have a large number of past jobs, summarize the earliest with a statement like: "1970–80, A variety of drafting positions."

6. Eliminate extraneous information. Employers don't need to know your weight, height, sex, marital status, health, children's names, church affiliations, social clubs, or fraternities. If and when they need the information (that which is legal), they will get it in the interview or application, or later.

7. Condense. Don't give three examples when one will suffice.

ACTION AND ACCOMPLISHMENTS

Most resumes make dull reading—a sure cure for even the severest cases of insomnia. The problem: a limp narrative style that focuses on routine duties and responsibilities and ends up sounding like descriptions from a civil service job announcement. Puts people to sleep. What keeps employers awake are words and phrases that create pictures they can see in their mind's eye. Word pictures.

To create vivid word pictures that will keep potential employers awake, you need to combine two prime ingredients: *active verbs* to start sentences and paragraphs, and descriptions of the *results* you have produced in the work you have done, rather than just the duties you have performed.

For example:

Limp style: My duties included doing promotion for customers and in-house incentive programs. I used a database to locate sources. These gave us a 20% gain in income.

Action style: Developed and managed customer promotions and sales incentive programs. Managed a database to provide sourcing information. Increased revenues by 20%.

An accomplishment is nothing more than a *result*, a final measurable product that people can relate to. A duty is not a result, it is an obligation —every job-holder has duties. What really scores are the *results*, the accomplishments. Use as many as you can in your resume, or in any communication you make about yourself in your job campaign.

You have produced results in many aspects of your life—school, church, homelife, hobbies. Use everything you can find to demonstrate that you are in fact a *producer*, not just another dutiful worker.

And start sentences with action verbs to stimulate the reader's appetite to learn more about you.

Here are some of the things that contemporary employers tell us they like to see:

- Work on a team.
- Energize and motivate others.
- Learn and use new things.
- Demonstrate versatility.
- Challenge old ways of thinking.
- Understand how profits are created.
- Display business savvy.
- Communicate directly and clearly, both written and verbal.
- Take risks.
- Admit mistakes.
- Manifest high personal standards.

Remember to couch your descriptions in terms that relate to specific or typical employer concerns. Every entry should be structured to reinforce your next job goal.

EXERCISE YOUR POWER WRITING SKILLS

Below is a sample list of personal power words. Go down the lists and check those you feel could be used in sentences or paragraphs to describe *your* accomplishments.

Personal Power Words

Created	Wrote	Referred
Instructed	Analyzed	Served
Reduced (losses)	Produced	Compounded
Negotiated	Conducted	Networked
Planned	Delivered	Observed
Sold	Founded	Studied
Completed	Assisted	Improved
Designed	Leveraged	Consolidated
Consulted	Increased	Ordered
Evaluated	Trained	Invented
Calculated	Supplied	Diagnosed
Identified	Maintained	Examined
Performed	Administered	Lectured
Constructed	Advised	Processed
Controlled	Restored	Reviewed

Dispensed	Criticized	Translated
Formulated	Realized	Prescribed
Improved	Rewarded	Charted
Tested	Purchased	Represented
Protected	Oversaw	Promoted
Obtained	Installed	Recorded
Programmed	Routed	Operated
Rendered	Corresponded	Supervised
Instructed	Audited	Drew up
Counseled	Coordinated	Organized
Received	Researched	Strategized
Built	Implemented	Expanded
Detected	Presented	Devised
Selected	Instituted	Prepared
Logged	Directed	Interpreted
Recommended	Managed	Interviewed
Distributed	Eliminated	Discovered
Arranged	Provided	Conserved
Disproved	Solved	Arbitrated
Developed	Determined	Assembled
Edited	Collected	Navigated
Acquired		

If there are any action words that clearly apply to you and are not on our list, add them.

_____

_____

_____

POWER PARAGRAPHS

Now take the job attractors and personal power words you have selected and, starting with each, write a short paragraph or long sentence describing a personal or work-related accomplishment or result you have produced. Do a minimum of three.

Power word or phrase: _____

_____

_____

_____

Power word or phrase: _____

_____

_____

_____

_____

Power word or phrase: _____

_____

_____

_____

_____

Go back over these power paragraphs now and see if they can be edited to increase impact. Can you cut words without reducing interest?

RESUME-WRITING TIPS

- Keep sentences and paragraphs *short* (no paragraph of more than ten lines).
- Use indented and "bulleted" statements (with • or * before each) where appropriate rather than complete sentences.
- Use simple terms rather than complex expressions that say the same thing.
- Use quantities, amounts, dollar values where they enhance the description of what you did ("increased sales by $100,000 per year").
- Put strongest statements at the top, working downward from them.
- Have someone with good English skills check for spelling, punctuation, and grammar.
- Do not use "I." It is implied throughout.
- Do not include hobbies or avocational or social interests unless they clearly contribute to your work ability for your current job target.
- Avoid self-serving evaluations.
- "I am an intelligent and diligent researcher" is to be avoided. "I completed three major research projects" would be included.
- Don't go overboard with esoteric jargon. Remember that the unenlightened may have to understand you, too.

Some Resume Don'ts

- Don't include pictures.
- Don't list references or relatives.
- Don't put resume in fancy binders or folders.
- Don't forget phone number, area code, zip.
- Don't list sex, weight, health, or other personal irrelevancies.
- Don't highlight problems (divorce, hospitalization, handicaps).
- Don't include addresses of prior employers (city and state are okay).
- Don't include salary information.

Final Reminders

Remember that the reason employers get interested in you is the value you can produce for them. This value is demonstrated by what you have done as much as by what you can do. Eliminate things that don't focus on your potential value. Above all, remember that your resume is a demonstration of your ability to handle written communication. Put as much care and attention into it as you would for a one-page advertisement for a fine product.

STEP 3: THE FACTS

To repeat: the purpose of your resume is to create enough interest to warrant an interview. It is a concise advertisement of your ability to create value and results: Your "history" is not the *primary* concern, it's your ability to get the job done.

Facts are not capabilities, as many a disappointed employer has learned. The fact that you have put in five years with another firm doing a particular task doesn't ensure your performance on the next job. With an increasing reluctance of employers to give other than perfunctory references for past employees, the *fact* of employment may only mean that's where you hung your hat and collected your paycheck.

However, the *facts* must be there, and reflected accurately and appropriately in a way that supports your capabilities.

On the following pages we are going to ask you to complete an inventory that describes important facts about yourself.

Full-time jobs

Part-time jobs

Education and training

Community work

Homework

Technical know-how

Projects completed

Hobbies

Honors and awards

References

When you have completed this self inventory, you probably will have collected more information than you *or* most employers are interested in knowing. That's how it should be. We believe in accumulating a large data base of information and then reducing and distilling what you've got into the key points. Be willing to take the extra time to complete it all. It will come in handy now and in the future—for resumes *and* employment applications.

YOUR RESUME INVENTORY

Fill out the following inventory of factual information. Not all of it may be required in your resume, but the information could be helpful to take with you to an interview or to fill out an application.

Education and Training

• *High School* •

If you are a college graduate, you will probably not use this information on your resume, but you could need it for application forms.

School _____

Dates attended _____ to _____ Graduated _____

Major studies _____ Class standing _____

Honors and awards _____

Best subjects _____

Jobs held while in high school and during summers _____

_____

Other achievements and activities _____

_____

_____

• *College (undergraduate)* •

School _____

Dates attended _____ to _____ Graduated _____

Major studies _____ Class standing _____

Honors and awards _____

Best subjects _____

Extracurricular activities _____

_____

Jobs held while in college and during summers _____

_____

Other achievements and activities _____

_____

_____

• *College (postgraduate, law school, medical school, etc.)* •

School _____

Dates attended _____ to _____ Graduated _____

School _____

Dates attended _____ to _____ Graduated _____

Major studies _____ Class standing _____

Honors and awards _____

Best subjects _____

Extracurricular activities _____

_____

Jobs held while in graduate school and during summers _____

_____

Other achievements and activities _____

_____

_____

On-Job and Employer-Sponsored Training

List any vocational courses, on-job training, military, or other formal training.

Course _____ Date taken _____

Skills learned _____

_____

Course _____ Date taken _____

Skills learned _____

Course _____ Date taken _____

Skills learned _____

_____

Licenses or certificates held _____

_____

Home and Community Work

Activities you have done at home for self and family that demonstrate your abilities. *Don't undervalue this experience.*

Accomplishment _____

Skills demonstrated _____

Accomplishment _____

Skills demonstrated _____

Accomplishment _____

Skills demonstrated _____

Hobbies

These reveal skills as well.

Hobby or activity _____

Accomplishment _____

Skills demonstrated _____

Hobby or activity _____

Accomplishment _____

Skills demonstrated _____

Part-Time Jobs

Job name _____ From/to _____

Employer/division _____

Accomplishments _____

Skills demonstrated _____

_____

Job name _____ From/to _____

Employer/division _____

Accomplishments _____

Skills demonstrated _____

_____

Full-Time Employment

List each major position held even if several are with same employer. Be sure to include *at least one* accomplishment for each position. (Note: You should start with your earliest and work up to most recent even though this order will be reversed if you do a chronological resume.)

19 _____ to _____ Position and title _____

Employer _____ Location _____

Accomplishments _____

Supervisor _____

19 _____ to _____ Position and title _____

Employer _____ Location _____

Accomplishments _____

Supervisor _____

19 _____ to _____ Position and title _____

Employer _____ Location _____

Accomplishments _____

Supervisor _____

19 _____ to _____ Position and title _____

Employer _____ Location _____

Accomplishments _____

Supervisor _____

Honors, Awards, Professional Societies, etc.

_____

_____

_____

_____

What Else?

List any other _factual_ information that demonstrates your skills, abilities, interests, accomplishments, or achievements.

_____

_____

_____

_____

References

Think in advance of the names and addresses of at least five people (professional preferred) who will give you a good and credible reference. (This will not be printed on your resume, but you will need it.)

_____

_____

_____

_____

_____

STEP 4: WRITING YOUR RESUME

Now it's time to pull it all together—all of the self-analysis, job targeting, writing practice, and factual inventory—into your own perfect resume, designed to stimulate employer interest and enthusiasm.

You will probably want to have a different version of your resume to cover each major area of employment search or job target. If you have two or three job targets, and they are in the same general work field, and you are using the chronological or functional format, then one version will suffice. If your job targets are reasonably diverse, then you will probably want one version for each target. If you are using the targeted resume, then you get maximum penetration by having a different resume for each target or work title.

In this part of the book we have provided work sheets, examples, and writing guides for each resume format. You need only concern yourself with those pages which relate to the format selected. Turn to that section now.

Chronological Resume	pages 72 to 81
Functional Resume	pages 81 to 89
Targeted Resume	pages 90 to 107
Resume Alternative	pages 107 to 111
Creative Alternative	pages 111 to 112

COMPUTING YOUR FUTURE

The power of the ubiquitous personal computer, word processor, and now the advent of special software for computer generation give you advantages that were rare even a few years ago. Basic word processing alone can cut in half the time for editing, revising, customizing, and updating old or basic resumes. There are many supports you will find right there in your standard word processor:

- Keeping a "stockpile" of powerful resume paragraphs on disk which can be cut and pasted in a variety of combinations to emphasize particular accomplishments or experience.

- Adding new accomplishments or experience as you get it.

- Trying out your resume in a variety of formats, fonts, bolds, underlines, left- or right-hand justification, etc., to review—one against the other—in order to contrast, compare, and choose the right one for the job at hand.

- Editing to fit one page.

- Spell-checking and thesaurus of synonyms.
- Revising in order to expand certain sections over others.
- Using a laser printer for top-quality appearance.
- Keeping a disk-based copy.

SOFTWARE FOR RESUMES

Over the past few years we have seen powerful new popular-priced software dedicated to the crafting of top-quality resumes. Going beyond regular word processors, most of these programs simplify the choice of layouts and style and provide power word vocabularies, sample phrases, and processes to help you assess your strengths and key capabilities—and allow the change of layout or format with the tap of a function key.

Some of the programs (our *Perfect Resume Computer Kit*™, for one) coach you with vision and targeting processes, provocative questions that simulate the job interview, routines that help critique the resume, and multiple storing and filing capability.

You don't need a computer program to write a good resume. This book and your willingness to do the headwork will suffice. Where you might want to consider resume software is where you plan to make your resumes super targeted or customized for different applications. If you are not that sharp with word processing, the resume packages—due to their formatting routines—will cut down the typing and organizing. Even if you don't have your own computer, by owning your own software disk and having access to a school or library computer, you gain a certain amount of portability in that you will take the disk with you and can continually upgrade it on other computers in your future.

Since new programs often change several times in their first few years, it can be improvident to recommend one over another. Check with your own software shop or counseling office.

PREPARING THE CHRONOLOGICAL RESUME

You have chosen the chronological resume to highlight a good work history related directly to your next job target, without major gaps or numerous job changes.

Rules for the Chronological Resume

1. Start with present or most recent position and work backward, with most space devoted to recent employment.

2. Detail only the last four or five positions or employment covering the last ten or so years. Summarize early positions unless exceptionally relevant to the present.

3. Use year designations, not month and day. Greater detail can be given in the interview or application.

4. You don't need to show every major position change with a given employer. List the most recent or present and two or three others at the most.

5. Do not repeat details that are common to several positions.

6. Within each position listed stress the *major* accomplishments and responsibilities that demonstrate your full competency to do the job. Once the most significant aspects of your work are clear, it is generally not necessary to include lesser achievements, as they will be assumed by employers.

7. Keep your *next job target* in mind, and as you describe prior positions and accomplishments emphasize those that are most related to your next move up.

8. Education is not included in chronological order. If it is within the past five years, it should go at the top of the resume. If earlier than that, at the bottom. (This is not a hard and fast rule, however, and you can follow your own instincts whether to emphasize work or education.)

9. And, of course, keep it to one page.

CHRONOLOGICAL

CORPORATE TRAINING MANAGER

Marsha M. Grant
198 Francis Avenue
Oklahoma City, OK 73109
405-824-6858

WORK EXPERIENCE:

1981 to Present — GRANNETT CORP., OKLAHOMA CITY, OK
Corporate Training Manager:
- Directed staff of ten trainers in three company locations.
- Consulted with senior management to determine training needs.
- Delegated design, development, and implementation process for four new courses.
- Managed $ 1.2 million budget.
- Evaluated results of 800 employees who attended programs.
- Devised an experimental curriculum on career planning.

1981-1984 — SIMON & CO., OKLAHOMA CITY, OK
Training Consultant
- Designed and developed technical and management development training programs.
- Delivered programs, workshops, and seminars to over a dozen groups of junior and middle managers.

1979 -1981 — PUBLIC SCHOOL SYSTEM, OKLAHOMA CITY, OK
Adult Education Training Assistant
- Taught classes for adults in liberal arts subjects.
- Selected programs and designed curriculum for English Department.

PROFESSIONAL SOCIETIES:
AMERICAN SOCIETY FOR TRAINING AND DEVELOPMENT

EDUCATION:
1984 — M.A. in Organizational Development
OKLAHOMA CITY UNIVERSITY

1979 — B.A. - UNIVERSITY OF OKLAHOMA

Chronological Resume Drafting Forms

• Instructions •

On the pages that follow, we have provided drafting forms that can be used to prepare your chronological resume. There are four such forms, each of which can be used to condense information relevant to a particular position or employer.

First, look over your resume inventory on pages 65–70 and select those positions you wish to include in your resume. Write these in the spaces provided below. Try to keep to five or fewer past positions in your resume.

Starting with the most recent position on the top of the drafting form, list everything you can think of relating to that job that you accomplished (check pages 68–69 for some reminders). Keep working until you have *filled* the top section with job related results you have produced.

Do this with each position you have selected. Then, look over all of the information on the top of the sheets and underline, or highlight, the activities in each position you feel are most indicative of your abilities and *most related to the next step in your career.*

In the space at the bottom of the drafting form, rewrite the information you have underscored into a concise and well-written paragraph or two that can be used in your resume.

> *For example, here is a paragraph as it appears* **before** *and* **after:**

Before:

I was responsible for trying to develop new business with banks in the U.S. I sold cash management and loan participation products and made five million dollars for the division.

After:

Marketed loan and cash management products to U.S. Financial Institutions. Generated revenues of $5 million.

CHRONOLOGICAL RESUME DRAFTING FORM (SAMPLE)

Dates _____ *1986* _____ to _____ *Present* _____ Position _____ *Assistant Director, Community Svcs.* _____

Employer _____ *Edison Township Community Board* _____

In the space below list as many accomplishments or results you can think of that describe your performance in the above position.

_____ *budget preparation — $800 K* _____

program development - S & S
proposal for government grant
approval $5000
legal liaison
oversee administrative staff

Underline the activities above you feel are most pertinent to your next job target, and rewrite below in condensed form suitable for your resume.

Prepared and managed annual budget of $800,000. Developed safety and security program for the elderly. Designed proposal and secured approval for $5000 government grant. Directed administrative staff of fire. Acted as liaison with attorneys interpreting government regulations.

CHRONOLOGICAL RESUME DRAFTING FORM, EMPLOYER #1

(Start with most recent employer.)

Dates _____ to _____ Position _____

Employer/Division _____ Location _____

In the space below list as many accomplishments or results you can think of that describe your performance in the above position.

_____

_____

_____

_____

_____

_____

_____

_____

_____

_____

Underline the activities above you feel are most pertinent to your next job target, and rewrite below in a condensed form suitable for your resume.

_____

_____

_____

_____

_____

CHRONOLOGICAL RESUME DRAFTING FORM, EMPLOYER #2

Dates _____ to _____ Position _____

Employer/Division _____ Location _____

In the space below list as many accomplishments or results you can think of that describe your performance in the above position.

_____

_____

_____

_____

_____

_____

_____

_____

_____

_____

_____

Underline the activities above you feel are most pertinent to your next job target, and rewrite below in a condensed form suitable for your resume.

_____

_____

_____

_____

_____

_____

CHRONOLOGICAL RESUME DRAFTING FORM, EMPLOYER #3

Dates _____ to _____ Position _____

Employer/Division _____ Location _____

In the space below list as many accomplishments or results you can think of that describe your performance in the above position.

_____

_____

_____

_____

_____

_____

_____

_____

_____

_____

_____

Underline the activities above you feel are most pertinent to your next job target, and rewrite below in a condensed form suitable for your resume.

_____

_____

_____

_____

_____

_____

_____

CHRONOLOGICAL RESUME DRAFTING FORM, EMPLOYER #4

Dates _____ to _____ Position _____

Employer/Division _____ Location _____

In the space below list as many accomplishments or results you can think of that describe your performance in the above position.

_____

_____

_____

_____

_____

_____

_____

_____

_____

Underline the activities above you feel are most pertinent to your next job target, and rewrite below in a condensed form suitable for your resume.

_____

_____

_____

_____

_____

_____

Note: Make additional copies of this form as necessary.

Assembly of Your Chronological Resume

You have now completed all of the information blocks for your chronological resume. Now assemble it into a fresh draft. Follow these steps:

1. Review the various chronological layouts in the sample resumes section (pages 135–189). Decide which layout appeals to you most and use this as a guide.

2. Start with a fresh sheet of paper, or turn on your word processor or computer, and type or write your name, address, zip code, and phone number (with area code). If your education is within the past five years, put it next after your address block. If previously, include it at the bottom.

3. Transcribe the date/position employer information and the condensed paragraphs from the bottom of each of the resume drafting forms you have just completed. Start with most recent employer first.

4. After you have assembled all information on the first draft, matching the sample you chose, check it over very carefully for omissions, irrelevancies, inaccuracies, and length. Make whatever corrections or additions you feel are required for the strongest personal presentation of yourself on one page.

5. Have several copies of a second draft typed from the first, incorporating all changes. This is where the computer will be very helpful. You should spell check and check the thesaurus for word choices. You can cut and paste several versions once you have the text cleaned up. Always look for simplicity and impact.

Present these copies to others for feedback and editing. They should be very close to the way you expect your final resume to look. Cut it back as necessary to fit one page (see pages 59 and 60 for tips on fitting on one page).

6. Final Critique. This is the last step before the final typing and printing—the final sign-off of a most important document. Decide on someone (or preferably several people) you feel you can trust to provide you with critical feedback. Give these people copies of the version you have chosen as your final draft and ask them to go over it with you and point out any areas where it can be improved. Use the checklist provided as a guide.

Chronological Resume Checklist

YES NO

____ ____ Are there any typing or spelling errors? (check twice)

____ ____ Are all statements easily understood?

____ ____ Is writing style concise and direct?

____ ____ Are paragraphs and sentences short and to the point?

_____ _____ Have redundancies and repetitions been eliminated?

_____ _____ Does each position demonstrate easily understood accomplishments?

_____ _____ Are all major relevant time periods covered?

_____ _____ Has all unnecessary information been eliminated?

_____ _____ Is layout simple, professional and attractive?

_____ _____ Does resume present best possible picture of candidate?

PREPARING THE FUNCTIONAL RESUME

By selecting the Functional Resume format, you have chosen to highlight particular areas of capability in order of highest relevance and potential rather than stay with your chronological work history. By doing this you will be able to point toward selected career directions and play down possible gaps or inconsistencies in past work. If you are changing careers, entering or reentering the job market, you have chosen an approach that will also allow you to easily talk about nonpaying work experience and school or community activities.

Sample List of Functional Headings

Check off the functions below that best describe your abilities and potential and are in line with your job target. Add any others that are appropriate. Narrow the list to four or five top choices and use these on your functional resume.

Accounting	Community Affairs	Fine Arts
Advertising	Computers	Fund Raising
Aeronautics	Construction	Graphic Design
Arbitrage	Consulting	Health Services
Architecture	Counseling	Horticulture
Automotive	Data Processing	Human Resources
Banking	Drafting	Industrial Design
Biology	Ecology	Insurance
Botany	Economics	Interior Design
Career	Education	Journalism
Development	Electronics	Law
Chemistry	Engineering	Layout
Child Care	Entertainment	Management
Coaching	Family Services	Marketing
Commercial Art	Fashion	Mathematics
Communications	Financial Planning	Medicine

Mental Health   Physics   Social Services
Movies   Planning   Sports
Museum Work   Printing   Strategic Planning
Music   Product Development Systems Design
Navigation   Programming   Television
News Anchor   Promotion   Textiles
Nutrition   Public Relations   Training
Oceanography   Public Service   Transportation
Office Services   Publishing   Travel
Organizational   Real Estate   Weather
  Development   Recreation   Word Processing
Performing Arts   Robotics   Writing and Editing
Photography   Sales
Physical Fitness   Secretarial

Additional functions not included in our list:

_____   _____

_____   _____

_____   _____

Rules for the Functional Resume

1. Use four or five separate paragraphs or sections, each one headlining a particular area of expertise or involvement (see sample page 83).

2. List the functional paragraphs in order of importance, with the area most related to your present job target at the top and containing slightly more information.

3. Within each functional area stress the most directly related accomplishments or results you have produced or the most powerful abilities (see pages 38 and 39).

4. Know that you can include any relevant accomplishment without necessarily identifying which employment or nonemployment situation it was connected to.

5. Include education toward the bottom, unless it was within the past three to five years. If it was in an unrelated field, include it at the end regardless of how recent.

6. List a brief synopsis of your actual work experience at the bottom, giving dates, employer, and title. If you have had no work experience or a very spotty record, leave out the employment synopsis entirely (but be prepared to talk about the subject at the interview).

7. And keep the length to one page.

Colin Richards
2346 Broadway
New York, NY 10025
(212) 662-4743

(2) VIDEO ENGINEERING:

° Manage quality control in production and post-production.
° Coordinate video content of news broadcasts, soap operas, and special events.
(3) ° Operate and maintain studio equipment including BVE 5000 editors, BVH 2000, BVU 800, and
BVW 10 machines.
° Supervise design and installation of a state of the art interformat online edit suite.
° Perform live, on-air switching and creation of video effects.

(1) SUPERVISION AND MANAGEMENT:

° Assign and manage all studio projects.
° Supervise and train video technicians.
° Evaluate all new potential equipment purchases.
° Interface with all production operations divisions.

EDITING:

° Supervise machine-to-machine edits, dubbing, and screening.
° Edit and reformat programs.
(4) ° Instruct members of NABET Local 15 in videotape editing.

PROFESSIONAL STANDING: FCC First Class License

(6) EXPERIENCE:

1986 to Present	American Broadcasting Co., New York, NY
	Senior Video Engineer
1982-1986	Carob Video, New York, NY
	Director of Engineering Operations
1980-1982	Video Planning, Inc., New York, NY
	Videotape Editor

(5) EDUCATION:

| 1980 | RCA Television Institute, New York, NY |
| 1979 | New York Institute of Technology, B.F.A. |

Functional Resume Drafting Forms

• Instructions •

On the following pages we have provided three special forms with which to draft your functional resume. Use them as noted.

Review the description on pages 38 and 39 of your skills. Check the sample list of functional categories above, and add any that relate to your capability or potential and also to your job target.

Select the five most powerful functions and list them in order of relevance on the tops of the forms that follow.

FUNCTIONAL RESUME DRAFTING FORM (SAMPLE 1)

Function title: _Physical Fitness_

In the space below, write down all achievements, accomplishments, or results *of any kind* that you have produced in your work experience, nonwork experience, school, or community activities. Don't go below the dotted line. (You can review pages 33–37 for ideas.)

I was responsible for teaching swimming to about 20 5-8 year olds at a local day camp. I volunteered to lead a lunch-hour workout group at my company for all the secretaries. Got company approval. While pregnant myself, I set up and ran exercise groups for pregnant and post-partum women in my community hall. I ran the Boston Marathon in 3 hours 13 minutes and helped 2 others to train for it. I studied and learned to use the Nautilus equipment at my health club.

Go over what you have written above, underline or highlight the most relevant information, and condense in the space provided a concise, effective resume paragraph. (See writing rules on pages 57–64.)

Instructed 20 young children in swimming. Obtained approval for, organized and managed a daily workout group for one firm's secretarial staff. Developed program for and instructed exercise groups for pregnant and post-partum women. Assisted 2 others in training for the Boston Marathon and successfully completed it in 3 hours.

FUNCTIONAL RESUME DRAFTING FORM (SAMPLE 2)

Function title: _Interior Design_

In the space below, write down all achievements, accomplishments, or results of *any kind* that you have produced in your work experience, nonwork experience, school, or community activities. Don't go below the dotted line.

Did plans for renovating interior of 1880's brownstone. Studied furniture & wallpaper from that period & found out where to get reproductions. I supervised the actual renovation. Later we sold the house for a 35% profit. Co-designed the interior of a new restaurant. Learned about building codes. Got all permits & approvals. Hired some special workers. Bought furniture. Ordered custom fabric & lighting.

Go over what you have written above, underline or highlight the most relevant information, and condense in the space provided a concise, effective resume paragraph.

Drew up plans and supervised interior renovation of 1880's brownstone. Researched period furnishings and wallcoverings and obtained reproductions. Sold house at 35% profit. Co-designed restaurant interior with attention to approvals + permits under city building codes. Hired sub-contractors. Purchased furnishings, custom fabric and lighting.

FUNCTIONAL RESUME DRAFTING FORM #1

Function title: _____

In the space below, write down all achievements, accomplishments, or results *of any kind* that you have produced in your work experience, nonwork experience, school, or community activities. Don't go below the dotted line. (You can review pages 33–37 for ideas.)

_____

_____

_____

_____

_____

_____

_____

_____

_____

....

Go over what you have written above, underline or highlight the most relevant information, and condense in the space provided a concise, effective resume paragraph. (See writing rules on pages 57–64.)

_____

_____

_____

_____

FUNCTIONAL RESUME DRAFTING FORM #2

Function title: _____

In the space below, write down all achievements, accomplishments, or results *of any kind* that you have produced in your work experience, nonwork experience, school, or community activities. Don't go below the dotted line.

_____

_____

_____

_____

_____

_____

_____

_____

_____

_____

....

Go over what you have written above, underline or highlight the most relevant information, and condense in the space provided a concise, effective resume paragraph.

_____

_____

_____

_____

_____

FUNCTIONAL RESUME DRAFTING FORM #3

Function title: _____

In the space below, write down all achievements, accomplishments, or results *of any kind* that you have produced in your work experience, nonwork experience, school, or community activities. Don't go below the dotted line.

_____

_____

_____

_____

_____

_____

_____

_____

_____

_____

. . . .

Go over what you have written above, underline or highlight the most relevant information, and condense in the space provided a concise, effective resume paragraph.

_____

_____

_____

_____

_____

Note: Make additional copies of this form as necessary.

Final Assembly of Your Functional Resume

You have completed all of the information development of your functional resume. Now pull it all together into a one-page masterpiece. The steps are simple:

1. Review the functional layouts in the sample resumes section (pages 135–189) and pick the one that appeals to you most. Use this as a guide.

2. Start with name, address, zip code, phone with area code. Education may be either at the top (if recent) or at the bottom. It may be emphasized or de-emphasized as you wish.

3. Transcribe the functional headings and condensed paragraphs from the resume drafting forms you have just completed.

4. After the functional descriptions, add a *brief* chronology of employment unless you feel that this would not be in your best interest.

5. Have several copies of a second draft typed from the first, incorporating all the changes. This is where the computer will be very helpful. You should spell check and check the thesaurus for word choices. You can cut and paste several versions once you have the text cleaned up. Always look for simplicity and impact.

Present these copies to others for feedback and editing. They should be very close to the way you expect your final resume to look. Cut it back as necessary to fit one page (see pages 59 and 60 for tips on fitting on one page).

6. Final Critique. This is the last step before the final typing and printing—the final sign-off of a most important document. Decide on someone (or preferably several people) you feel you can trust to provide you with critical feedback. Give these people copies of the version you have chosen as your final draft and ask them to go over it with you and point out any areas where it can be improved. Use the checklist provided as a guide.

Functional Resume Checklist

YES NO

____ ____ Are there any typing or spelling errors? (check twice)

____ ____ Are all statements easily understood?

____ ____ Is writing style concise and direct?

____ ____ Are paragraphs and sentences short and to the point?

____ ____ Have redundancies and repetitions been eliminated?

____ ____ Does each position demonstrate easily understood accomplishments?

____ ____ Are all major relevant time periods covered?

_____ _____ Has all unnecessary information been eliminated?
_____ _____ Is layout simple, professional and attractive?
_____ _____ Does resume present best possible picture of candidate?

Turn to pages 112 to 121 to learn about final word processing and production, and some valuable information about cover letters.

PREPARING THE TARGETED RESUME

With the first edition of this book, we introduced a brand new resume format designed to focus capabilities and accomplishments sharply toward a well-developed, future-focused job target. Unlike the chronological and functional resumes, which describe past work, the targeted resume features statements about what you can do—your capabilities—even if you have not actually had any direct relevant experience yet.

You are using the targeted resume because you are clear about a particular job target or targets (use a different resume for each) and your willingness to focus on these alone. The resume is actually quite simple to prepare, so it would not be difficult on a computer or word processor to put together three or four.

In using this format it is essential to research the fields you have chosen to target. Research is the trade-off for any lack of direct experience.

If you are interested in finding out more about your job target areas, a visit to your library is mandatory. Books, periodicals, reference works, trade publications, and bibliographies will give you insight and direction. Simply ask the librarian, and she can help you find out about what people do in this field, the jargon they use. You will then be able to express truly relevant capabilities that clearly support your targets.

Rules for the Targeted Resume

1. You must be clear about a specific job target (or targets if you plan several versions). A job target is a clear description of a particular title or occupational field that you want to pursue (see page 48 and those preceding).

2. The statements of capability and accomplishment must all be directly related to the job target. This may require some reading or research in the field.

3. Both capabilities and accomplishments will be short statements of one or two lines, generally written in an active style.

4. Listed capabilities will answer the underlying question, _"What can you do?"_ Listed accomplishments will answer the underlying question, _"What have you done?"_

5. Experience and education are listed but not openly stressed—they support rather than control.

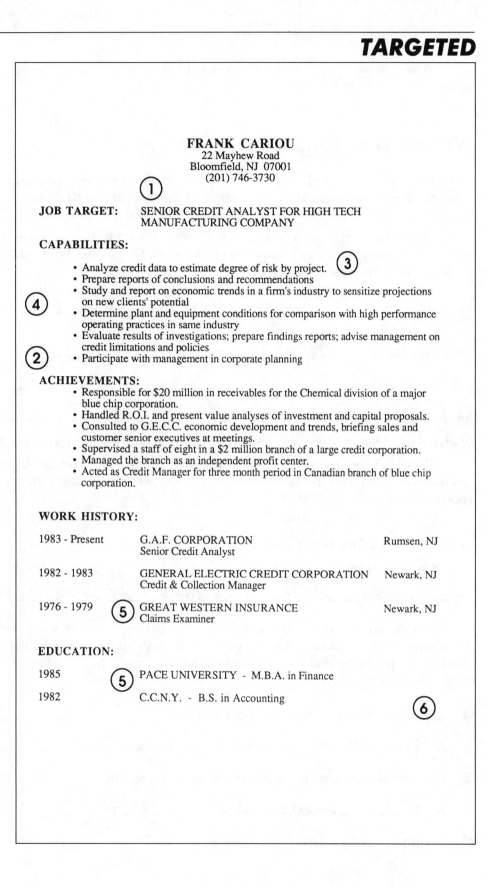

FRANK CARIOU
22 Mayhew Road
Bloomfield, NJ 07001
(201) 746-3730

①

JOB TARGET: SENIOR CREDIT ANALYST FOR HIGH TECH
MANUFACTURING COMPANY

CAPABILITIES:

③

- Analyze credit data to estimate degree of risk by project.
- Prepare reports of conclusions and recommendations
- Study and report on economic trends in a firm's industry to sensitize projections on new clients' potential

④

- Determine plant and equipment conditions for comparison with high performance operating practices in same industry
- Evaluate results of investigations; prepare findings reports; advise management on credit limitations and policies

②

- Participate with management in corporate planning

ACHIEVEMENTS:

- Responsible for $20 million in receivables for the Chemical division of a major blue chip corporation.
- Handled R.O.I. and present value analyses of investment and capital proposals.
- Consulted to G.E.C.C. economic development and trends, briefing sales and customer senior executives at meetings.
- Supervised a staff of eight in a $2 million branch of a large credit corporation.
- Managed the branch as an independent profit center.
- Acted as Credit Manager for three month period in Canadian branch of blue chip corporation.

WORK HISTORY:

1983 - Present	G.A.F. CORPORATION Senior Credit Analyst	Rumsen, NJ
1982 - 1983	GENERAL ELECTRIC CREDIT CORPORATION Credit & Collection Manager	Newark, NJ
1976 - 1979	⑤ GREAT WESTERN INSURANCE Claims Examiner	Newark, NJ

EDUCATION:

| 1985 | ⑤ PACE UNIVERSITY - M.B.A. in Finance |
| 1982 | C.C.N.Y. - B.S. in Accounting |

⑥

6. The resume should easily fit on one page with plenty of "white space."

Writing Your Targeted Resume

- Preparing a targeted resume is actually an easy process, since the substantive material essentially comes out of the answers to two basic questions about your job target(s): *What can you do?* and *What have you done?*

- Using the forms that follow, you will create fifteen to twenty statements of capability and of accomplishment for each target, and then boil these down to the most powerful.

- Start by writing down one, two, or three specific job targets below. They can be from the earlier pages of this book, or you can come up with others.

Job Target No. 1 _____

Job Target No. 2 _____

Job Target No. 3 _____

We have provided enough work sheets for you to produce these resumes.

- For each job target, complete one *capabilities work sheet* and one *accomplishments work sheet* and combine them in accordance with the sample format shown.

• *Capabilities Work Sheet (Sample)* •

(WHAT YOU *CAN* DO)

Sample Job Target ___*Sales / Customer Service Manager*___

Repeat each question to yourself and fill in the answer denoting what you *feel* or *think* you can do (whether or not you have done it) or could do in the performance of that job target. Continue to ask these questions until you are satisfied that you have a full list of at least twenty. Then select or rewrite the most powerful ten.

Q. Regarding your job target, what can you do?

A. I can ___*make sales forecasts*___

Q. Concerning your job target, list something else you can do.

A. I can ___*manage sales activities*___

Q. Regarding your job target, what else can you do?

A. I can _analyze market trends_

Q. In relation to your job target, list something you can do.

A. I can _determine budget and operate within it_

Q. What else is there that you can do related to your job target?

A. I can _motivate groups and individuals_

Q. Regarding your job target, what can you do that creates value?

A. I can _negotiate contracts_

Q. As regards your job target, what can you do that relates to money?

A. I can _generate cost-saving ideas_

Q. Regarding your job target, think of something else you can do.

A. I can _manage client relations_

Q. Regarding your job target, what could you do if you were willing to play 100 percent?

A. I could _conduct research for improved services_

Q. As regards your job target, what can you do that produces value for people?

A. I can _analyze competitors' products_

Q. List something else you can do that would be related to your job target.

A. I can _prepare employee appraisals_

Q. What would you be willing to do about your job target that would be valuable?

A. I would be willing to _monitor quality_

Q. What can you do in another field that could be related to your job target?

A. I can _compile reports and records_

Q. What else can you do that could be valuable in your job target objective?

A. I can _supervise others_

Q. What can you do in your nonwork life that could be applicable to your job target?

A. I can _manage projects_

Q. What other things can you do or could do that would be valuable in your job target?

A. I can _plan and maintain work schedules_

A. I could _control inventory._

A. I can _evaluate procedures and practices_

A. I could _plan advertising and promotions._

Don't stop this process until you have come up with at least twenty *I can*s or *I could*s. Remember that these don't need to be things you *have* done, just tasks that you feel confident you can or could do that would be valuable in your job target. Go over your list and put an X in front of ten of the capabilities you would like to include in your resume. And then complete the accomplishments work sheet. See page 106 for assembling instructions.

• Accomplishments Work Sheet (Sample) •

(WHAT YOU *HAVE* DONE)

Sample Job Target _Executive Search Consultant_

Read and answer each question with a short statement describing something tangible you have *done*. What results or accomplishments *from any area of your experience—work or nonwork—*that will illustrate or demonstrate your ability to produce results in your job target area. Continue to answer the questions until you have come up with at least twelve to fifteen "I haves," which can be reduced to eight for your resume.

Q. As regards your job target, what have you done?

A. I have _interviewed over 300 candidates_

Q. As regards your job target, what else have you done?

A. I have _Consulted with over 40 companies_

Q. As regards your job target, what else have you done?

A. I have _successfully placed over 100 candidates in management positions._

Q. What is something else you have done that relates to your job target?

A. I have _recruited 5 CEO's_

Q. As regards your job target, what result have you produced?

A. I have _generated additional 20% in fees over previous year_

Q. As regards your job target, what have you accomplished?

A. I have _brought in 6 new corporate clients this year_

Q. As regards your job target, list something you have achieved.

A. I have _trained candidates in effective interviewing techniques_

Q. Regarding your job target, list something you have done in another field that could be related.

A. I have _Conducted workshops on resume writing_

Q. Regarding your job target, list something you have done that you are proud of.

A. I have _encouraged several executives to start their own businesses_

Q. Regarding your job target what have you done that was valuable financially to someone else?

A. I have _advised a woman to negotiate & obtain a 40% salary increase_

Q. Regarding your job target, think of something tangible you have done.

A. I have _read over 1000 resumes_

Q. Identify something you have done in your private life that relates to your job target.

A. I have _supported others to be straightforward in communicating_

Q. Regarding your job target, what have you done that demonstrates an ability to work with people?

A. I have _coordinated with staff in 3 regional offices_

Q. Think of some other things you have done in work or nonwork-related experiences that demonstrate your ability to produce results?

A. I have _negotiated increased fees from clients_

A. I have _volunteered in an adult literacy program_

A. I have _chaired the Membership Committee of ASTD_

A. I have _published an article on executive recruiting_

Go back over all of the "I haves" you have listed and select eight of these for actual use in your resume. Put an X in front of each of these.

• Capabilities Work Sheet •

(WHAT YOU _CAN_ DO)

Job Target No. 1 _____

Repeat each question to yourself and fill in the answer denoting what you *feel* or *think* that you can do (whether or not you have done it) or could do in the performance of that job target. Continue to ask these questions until you are satisfied that you have a full list of at least twenty answers. Then select or rewrite the most powerful ten.

Q. Regarding your job target, what can you do?

A. I can _____

Q. Concerning your job target, list something else you can do.

A. I can _____

Q. Regarding your job target, what else can you do?

A. I can _____

Q. Regarding your job target, what can you do that creates value?

A. I can _____

Q. Related to your job target, what can you do that relates to money?

A. I can _____

Q. Regarding your job target, think of something else you can do.

A. I can _____

Q. Regarding your job target, what could you do if you were willing to play 100 percent?

A. I could _____

Q. Related to your job target, what can you do that produces value for people?

A. I can _____

Q. List something else you can do that would be related to your job target.

A. I can _____

Q. What would you be willing to do regarding your job target that would be valuable?

A. I would be willing to _____

Q. What can you do in another field that could be related to your job target?

A. I can _____

Q. What else can you do that could be valuable in your job target objective?

A. I can _____

Q. What can you do in your nonwork life that could be applicable to your job target?

A. I can _____

Q. What other things can you do or could you do that would be valuable in your job target?

A. I can _____

A. I could _____

A. I can _____

A. I could _____

Don't stop this process until you have come up with at least twenty *I can*s or *I could*s. Remember that these don't need to be things you *have* done, just tasks that you feel confident you can or could do that would be valuable in your job target. Go over your list and put an X in front of ten of the capabilities you would like to include in your resume. And then complete the accomplishments work sheet. See page 106 for assembling instructions.

• *Accomplishments Work Sheet* •

(WHAT YOU *HAVE* DONE)

Job Target No. 1 _____

Read and answer each question with a short statement describing something tangible you have *done*. What results or accomplishments *from any area of your experience—work or nonwork—*that will illustrate or demonstrate your ability to produce results in your job target area. Continue to answer the questions until you have come up with at least twelve to fifteen "I haves," which can be reduced to eight for your resume.

Q. Regarding your job target, what have you done?

A. I have _____

Q. Concerning your job target, what else have you done?

A. I have _____

Q. Regarding your job target, what else have you done?

A. I have _____

Q. What is something else you have done that relates to your job target?

A. I have _____

Q. Related to your job target, what result have you produced?

A. I have _____

Q. Regarding your job target, what have you accomplished?

A. I have _____

Q. Concerning your job target, list something you have done in another field that could be related.

A. I have _____

Q. Regarding your job target, list something you have done that you are proud of.

A. I have _____

Q. Regarding your job target, what have you done that was valuable financially to someone else?

A. I have _____

Q. Regarding your job target, think of something tangible you have done.

A. I have _____

Q. Identify something you have done in your private life that relates to your job target.

A. I have _____

Q. Regarding your job target, what have you done that demonstrates an ability to work with people?

A. I have _____

Q. Think of some other things you have done in work or nonwork-related experiences that demonstrate your ability to produce results.

A. I have _____

A. I have _____

A. I have _____

A. I have _____

Go back over all of the "I haves" you have listed and select eight of these for actual use in your resume. Put an X in front of these.

• Capabilities Work Sheet •

(WHAT YOU *CAN* DO)

Job Target No. 2 _____

Repeat each question to yourself and fill in the answer denoting what you *feel* or *think* that you can do (whether or not you have done it) or could do in the performance of that job target. Continue to ask these questions until you are satisfied that you have a full list of at least twenty. Then select or rewrite the most powerful ten.

Q. As regards your job target, what can you do?

   A. I can _____

Q. As regards your job target, list something else you can do.

   A. I can _____

Q. As regards your job target, what else can you do?

   A. I can _____

Q. In relation to your job target, list something you can do.

   A. I can _____

Q. What else is there that you can do related to your job target?

   A. I can _____

Q. As regards your job target, what can you do that creates value?

   A. I can _____

Q. As regards your job target, what can you do that relates to money?

   A. I can _____

Q. Regarding your job target, think of something else you can do.

   A. I can _____

Q. Regarding your job target, what could you do if you were willing to play 100 percent?

   A. I could _____

Q. As regards your job target, what can you do that produces value for people?

A. I can _____

Q. List something else you can do that would be related to your job target.

A. I can _____

Q. What would you be willing to do about your job target that would be valuable?

A. I would be willing to _____

Q. What can you do in another field that could be related to your job target?

A. I can _____

Q. What else can you do that could be valuable in your job target objective?

A. I can _____

Q. What can you do in your nonwork life that could be applicable to your job target?

A. I can _____

Q. What other things can you do or could do that would be valuable in your job target?

A. I can _____

A. I could _____

A. I can _____

A. I could _____

Don't stop this process until you have come up with at least twenty *I can*s or *I could*s. Remember that these don't need to be things you *have* done, just tasks that you feel confident you can or could do that would be valuable in your job target. Go over your list and put an X in front of ten of the capabilities you would like to include in your resume. And then complete the accomplishments work sheet.

• *Accomplishments Work Sheet* •

(WHAT YOU *HAVE* DONE)

Job Target No.2 _____

    Read and answer each question with a short statement describing something tangible you have *done*. What results or accomplishments *from any area of your experience—work or nonwork—*that will illustrate or demonstrate your ability to produce results in your job target area. Continue to answer the questions until you have come up with at least twelve to fifteen "I haves," which can be reduced to eight for your resume.

Q. As regards your job target, what have you done?

    A. I have _____

Q. As regards your job target, what else have you done?

    A. I have _____

Q. As regards your job target, what else have you done?

    A. I have _____

Q. What is something else you have done that relates to your job target?

    A. I have _____

Q. As regards your job target, what result have you produced?

    A. I have _____

Q. As regards your job target, what have you accomplished?

    A. I have _____

Q. As regards your job target, list something you have achieved.

    A. I have _____

Q. Regarding your job target, list something you have done in another field that could be related.

    A. I have _____

Q. Regarding your job target, list something you have done that you are proud of.

    A. I have _____

Q. Regarding your job target, what have you done that was valuable financially to someone else?

A. I have _____

Q. Regarding your job target, think of something tangible you have done.

A. I have _____

Q. Identify something you have done in your private life that relates to your job target.

A. I have _____

Q. Regarding your job target, what have you done that demonstrates an ability to work with people?

A. I have _____

Q. Think of some other things you have done in work or nonwork-related experiences that demonstrate your ability to produce results?

A. I have _____

A. I have _____

A. I have _____

A. I have _____

Go back over all of the "I haves" you have listed and select eight of these for actual use in your resume. Put an X in front of each of these.

• Capabilities Work Sheet •

(WHAT YOU *CAN* DO)

Job Target No. 3 _____

Repeat each question to yourself and fill in the answer denoting what you *feel* or *think* that you can do (whether or not you have done it) or could do in the performance of that job target. Continue to ask these questions until you are satisfied that you have a full list of at least twenty. Then select or rewrite the most powerful ten.

Q. As regards your job target, what can you do?

A. I can _____

Q. As regards your job target, list something else you can do.

A. I can _____

Q. As regards your job target, what else can you do?

A. I can _____

Q. In relation to your job target, list something you can do.

A. I can _____

Q. What else is there that you can do related to your job target?

A. I can _____

Q. As regards your job target, what can you do that creates value?

A. I can _____

Q. As regards your job target, what can you do that relates to money?

A. I can _____

Q. Regarding your job target, think of something else you can do.

A. I can _____

Q. Regarding your job target, what could you do if you were willing to play 100 percent?

A. I could _____

Q. As regards your job target, what can you do that produces value for people?

A. I can _____

Q. List something else you can do that would be related to your job target.

A. I can _____

Q. What would you be willing to do regarding your job target that would be valuable?

A. I would be willing to _____

Q. What can you do in another field that could be related to your job target?

A. I can _____

Q. What else can you do that could be valuable in your job target objective?

    A. I can _____

Q. What can you do in your nonwork life that could be applicable to your job target?

    A. I can _____

Q. What other things can you do or could do that would be valuable in your job target?

    A. I can _____

    A. I could _____

    A. I can _____

    A. I could _____

Don't stop this process until you have come up with at least twenty *I can*s or *I could*s. Remember that these don't need to be things you *have* done, just tasks that you feel confident you can or could do that would be valuable in your job target. Go over your list and put an X in front of ten of the capabilities you would like to include in your resume. And then complete the accomplishments work sheet.

• *Accomplishments Work Sheet* •

(WHAT YOU *HAVE* DONE)

Job Target No. 3 _____

Read and answer each question with a short statement describing something tangible you have *done*. What results or accomplishments *from any area of your experience—work or nonwork—*that will illustrate or demonstrate your ability to produce results in your job target area. Continue to answer the questions until you have come up with at least twelve to fifteen "I haves," which can be reduced to eight for your resume.

Q. As regards your job target, what have you done?

    A. I have _____

Q. As regards your job target, what else have you done?

    A. I have _____

Q. As regards your job target, what else have you done?

    A. I have _____

Q. What is something else you have done that relates to your job target?

A. I have _____

Q. As regards your job target, what result have you produced?

A. I have _____

Q. As regards your job target, what have you accomplished?

A. I have _____

Q. As regards your job target, list something you have achieved.

A. I have _____

Q. Regarding your job target, list something you have done in another field that could be related.

A. I have _____

Q. Regarding your job target, list something you have done that you are proud of.

A. I have _____

Q. Regarding your job target what have you done that was valuable financially to someone else?

A. I have _____

Q. Regarding your job target, think of something tangible you have done.

A. I have _____

Q. Identify something you have done in your private life that relates to your job target.

A. I have _____

Q. Regarding your job target, what have you done that demonstrates an ability to work with people?

A. I have _____

Q. Think of some other things you have done in work or nonwork-related experiences that demonstrate your ability to produce results?

A. I have _____

A. I have _____

A. I have _____

A. I have _____

Go back over all of the "I haves" you have listed and select eight of these for actual use in your resume. Put an X in front of each of these.

Final Assembly of Your Targeted Resume

As you will see from the resume samples (pages 135–189), layouts for the Targeted Resume are all essentially the same. The format has been designed for simplicity and directness.

The assembly of your resume is therefore quite easy.

1. Put name, address, zip code, and phone number (with area code) centered at the top.

2. List your specific job target next in all capital letters or by capitalizing the initial letter of each word.

3. Use the heading *Capabilities* (to describe what you *can do* for this target). You may follow this with a sentence such as: "In my job target area I am able to achieve the following:"

4. Under this heading list eight to ten brief capabilities statements selected from the prior work sheets. Start each of these with a (•) or (*) or (−) for emphasis and style.

5. Follow this with the heading *Accomplishments* (which illustrate what you have done). Include a lead-in statement such as "Listed below are some of the accomplishments related to my job target."

6. List five to six solid accomplishments from the appropriate work sheet in concise statements preceded by (•) or (*) or (−) for emphasis and style.

7. Follow this with the heading *Experience* and use no more than five lines to summarize your work history (dates, employer, title). If you have more positions to list than five lines will allow, combine earlier jobs in a statement such as: "1975–80 Held other commercial positions."

8. The final heading is *Education*. You should use only two or three lines to detail your most recent education—school, degree or program, dates.

9. When all the information is assembled, type—preferably on a word processor—a single-spaced draft to fit neatly on one page. If you have more space, you can add other capabilities or accomplishments. If you need to cut back, you can shorten or delete the least needed information. This is your final draft.

10.   Have one or more people you trust go over the resume and critique it for completeness, clarity, spelling, neatness, and organization. Encourage criticism.

11.   Make all corrections and adjustments.

You have finished the final draft of your Targeted Resume. If, as we suggest, you have two or three different job targets, you will want to go through the same procedure with your other targets. Using a computer will save you time and steps.

For instructions on the final typing and printing, turn to Step 5, Word Processing, Layout, and Production, pages 112–117.

PREPARING THE RESUME ALTERNATIVE

Use this format if you are in a situation where it is really not helpful to use a more traditional resume. For example, use it if you have been out of the labor force for a number of years (as with a homemaker who has had very few outside activities) or if all your experience has been in a job that is far removed from your new job target.

The resume alternative letter is a personalized communication to an individual potential employer and reflects a clear communication of what you can do for him/her or the firm in very specific terms. It looks forward, rather than backward, and very clearly and specifically answers the question, *Why should I hire you?*

It takes research—lots of it—to help you zero in on the particular activities of an employer to whom you can contribute. It also takes thorough introspection and self-analysis (the Career Discovery Process would be valuable) to be clear about what you can offer. The idea of this approach is to present enough about yourself and your ability to make a contribution to an employer, in unstructured form, so that there is no need for a traditional resume.

Rules for the Resume Alternative Letter

1.   Complete the Career Discovery Process at the beginning of this book if possible.

2.   Be very specific in choosing job targets.

3.   Identify several specific *employers*, and do enough research (see pages 205–209) so you learn exactly what you could do to be of real value to the person to whom you are sending the letter and wish to meet.

4.   In your letter, communicate enough basic factual information about yourself so a full resume is not really needed. Keep to one page.

5. Construct the letter so a "meeting" with the employer is the next natural step. Suggest a time and place.

6. Make each letter as professional appearing as possible—word processed, spell checked, proofread thoroughly, and on your own pre-printed letterhead stationery.

ADMINISTRATIVE COORDINATOR

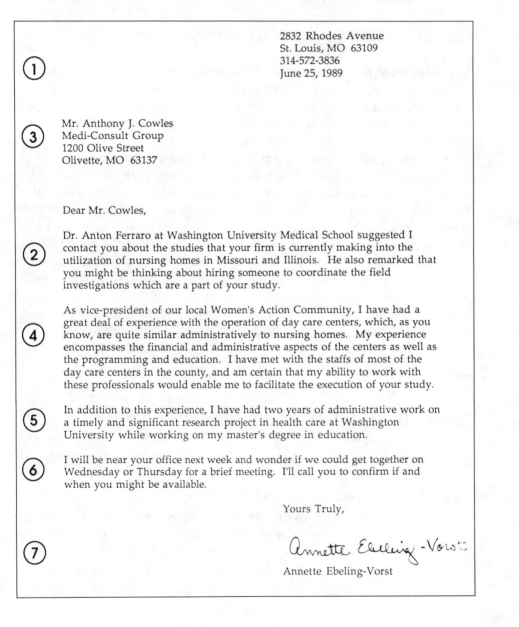

①
2832 Rhodes Avenue
St. Louis, MO 63109
314-572-3836
June 25, 1989

③
Mr. Anthony J. Cowles
Medi-Consult Group
1200 Olive Street
Olivette, MO 63137

Dear Mr. Cowles,

②
Dr. Anton Ferraro at Washington University Medical School suggested I contact you about the studies that your firm is currently making into the utilization of nursing homes in Missouri and Illinois. He also remarked that you might be thinking about hiring someone to coordinate the field investigations which are a part of your study.

④
As vice-president of our local Women's Action Community, I have had a great deal of experience with the operation of day care centers, which, as you know, are quite similar administratively to nursing homes. My experience encompasses the financial and administrative aspects of the centers as well as the programming and education. I have met with the staffs of most of the day care centers in the county, and am certain that my ability to work with these professionals would enable me to facilitate the execution of your study.

⑤
In addition to this experience, I have had two years of administrative work on a timely and significant research project in health care at Washington University while working on my master's degree in education.

⑥
I will be near your office next week and wonder if we could get together on Wednesday or Thursday for a brief meeting. I'll call you to confirm if and when you might be available.

Yours Truly,

⑦
Annette Ebeling-Vorst
Annette Ebeling-Vorst

• *Resume Alternative Letter* •

DRAFTING FORM #1

Prior to writing each alternative letter, fill out this form after doing as much research as you can (review pages 205–209).

EMPLOYER PROSPECT _____

Name and title of person to meet _____

Employer _____ Division or dept. _____

Address _____ Phone _____

What is your specific job target with this employer? Describe. _____

_____

What could you do for this employer that would create direct measurable value?

_____

_____

What else could you do? _____

_____

What can you say about *what you have done* that will *demonstrate* your ability to produce results for

the employer? _____

_____

Is there anything about your education or training (formal or informal) you can mention in your letter that will be relevant to what you want to do?

_____

_____

Is there any prior work activity (paid or unpaid) you should mention to demonstrate your fitness

for the job target? _____

_____

When would you like to meet with this employer? _____

_____

Is there any other directly relevant information that will help make the employer want to see you?

_____

_____

• *Resume Alternative Letter* •

DRAFTING FORM #2

Prior to writing each alternative letter, fill out this form, doing whatever research is necessary (review pages 205–209).

EMPLOYER PROSPECT _____

Name and title of person to meet _____

Employer _____ Division or dept. _____

Address _____ Phone _____

What is your specific job target with this employer? Describe.

_____

_____

What can you do for the employer that would create direct measurable value?

_____

_____

What else can you do? _____

_____

What can you say about *what you have done* that will *demonstrate* your ability to produce results for

the employer? _____

_____

Is there anything about your education or training (formal or informal) you can mention in your letter that will be relevant to what you want to do? _____

_____

Is there any prior work activity (paid or unpaid) you should mention to demonstrate your fitness

for the job target? _____

_____

When would you like to meet with this employer? _____

_____

Is there any other directly relevant information that will help make the employer want to see you?

_____

_____

PREPARING THE CREATIVE ALTERNATIVE RESUME

A Creative Alternative Resume is a highly stylized message that expresses your creativity in an unusual way.

The first rule about the creative alternative is *not* to take this approach unless you are truly able to put together a level of communication that works creatively in *the eyes of others*—and will be so interpreted by the person to whom it is directed. Resume readers are skeptical, and the line between creativity and gimmickry can be very obvious to them.

The creative alternative is more of a demonstration than a description of what you can do. Some of the career situations in which we have seen it used effectively are:

- Advertising copywriter (a well-written ad for oneself)
- Greeting card illustrator (oneself as subject of card)
- Magazine illustrator (cartoon strip about oneself)
- New product manager (a "self as product" description)
- Model (montage of photos—details on back)
- Actor (picture and copies of reviews)
- Fund raiser (letter "soliciting" an interview)

For each creative alternative we have seen work, there are five that have fallen flat. Here are some pointers to consider if this approach appeals to you.

- Consider preparing a more conventional resume as a backup.
- Make sure that what you do is very professionally produced or reproduced.
- Make the results look effortless—not a grind.
- Favor brevity and simplicity.
- Make sure the point is made: a personal meeting is called for.

We have not provided samples of the creative alternatives, since there is no pattern to follow. In this one, you are in the writer's seat.

STEP 5: WORD PROCESSING, LAYOUT, AND PRODUCTION

Before that resume of yours is seriously read by anyone in the employment cycle, it has to pass what we call the *flash test*—that first three- to four-second look in which the reader decides whether or not it's worth reading any further. This is analogous to the way that you yourself might scan pages of a newspaper or magazine to decide which articles or advertisements are worth reading.

Unfortunately, in this unfair employment world of ours, skills just aren't enough—packaging counts. Employers and consultants agree that many able candidates don't make it beyond the initial screening process due to poorly constructed, poorly presented resumes. The underlying assumption is that, if you can't communicate about yourself in a way that invites interest and attention, you aren't fully equipped to deal with today's highly communications-oriented work world. Like it or not, that's the way it is.

But of course *you* don't really need to worry, since, having reached this stage of your resume development, you can proceed to the final packaging with confidence and clarity.

The following packaging steps have been pretested and refined from several lifetimes of resume reading and writing by employment and counseling experts. We recommend that you follow them as exactly as you can. As you follow these final steps, remember what we said many pages back —that your resume not only *describes*, it also *demonstrates* your ability to handle basic written communication.

DESKTOP RESUME PUBLISHING

Just a few years ago this section would be about typewriters, offset printing, and typesetting. Fortunately, today we are able to talk about one of the most significant aids to the resume preparer—the word processor and/or, specifically, the home/personal computer. The enormous expansion of these tools has put before everyone the opportunity to produce high-production, high-quality resume output from their computers or word processors.

Even though you don't have these resources, access through libraries and counseling centers is high; and by utilizing these tools you'll be able to produce customized, targeted, high-quality resumes, which both simplifies and expands your ability to communicate to employers.

If you don't yet have access to computers or dedicated word processors, don't worry. You're still very much in the running and can easily produce the highest competitive-quality resumes.

(If you have access to *The Perfect Resume Computer Kit*™ [see page 5] you will already have many of the following choices available to you in the program itself.)

By knowing the basics of your word processor, or working with someone who does, you can accomplish the following:

- Store a large number of key paragraphs and phrases related to capabilities and accomplishments and other data. This will allow you to put together a variety of versions or formats of your resume and to strategically determine which approach is best for any given situation.
- Edit easily and quickly.
- Adjust your length to stay in line with the one-page rule.
- Use the spell-checker and/or thesaurus to help get the words right and appropriate.
- Keep copies of resumes that went to specific employers.
- Experiment with a variety of approaches.
- Constantly up-date and keep current.
- Print a perfect resume whenever you choose to.

TYPING AND TYPOGRAPHY

To prepare your resume for duplication, find the best word processor or professional typewriter you can within your area. Don't skimp on this. If you have to rent either, or pay someone to type your resume in order to get the best, don't hesitate to do so. With all that you have invested in the process to date, this is no place to start cutting back.

Follow these simple typing rules:

- Use a clear, dark typewriter ribbon (preferable cartridge).
- Make sure the name, address, and phone number are centered on the top.
- Use one-inch margins, minimum, on all sides.
- Don't make it look cramped—use plenty of white space.
- Highlight important titles by using caps and underlining.
- Use single space—double between paragraphs.

It is not advisable to have your entire resume professionally typeset by a printer or typesetter, as this is usually seen as graphic overkill and shows insecurity. It is all right to set type for major headings and name and address, to highlight these areas. Most printers will be able to do this for you at a reasonable cost. Bold headings can also be put in with typewriters that have changeable type elements. It's your own choice how much attention to pay to these areas. Review our samples (pages 135–189). Of course, word processing will give you an excellent selection of typefaces, as well as easily accessed bold print.

WHITE SPACE

One thing you will notice about most good advertising layouts is the conscious use of empty space on the page, known in the ad trade as "air" or white space. It serves as a way of accenting what is on the page in a way that is restful on the eye and mind. It implies that you are confident enough in what you have to say that you don't need to fill every space. Create white space in your resume through wide margins, double spacing between major paragraphs, careful positioning of your name and address block, and use of indentions. Caution: Don't put in so much air that there isn't much else. Use our samples as guides for your own layout.

LAYOUT

The purpose of the layout, or organization of your resume, is to attract the reader's eye to the most powerful parts, and to make it effortless for the reader to get the picture you wish to describe. A good layout is unobtrusive yet directs the eye unconsciously to the important parts. Some of the elements of your layout that you can work with are:

• UPPER CASE LETTERS—For headings or titles that are important. Use sparingly, as overuse tends to cancel out. Be consistent.

• Underlining—Can be used in the body of the resume to emphasize a dramatic result, accomplishment, or other highlight that you want the employer to see. Be careful that what you underline is, in fact, special, because if the reader doesn't agree, then the whole idea backfires. Also, use underlining sparingly, as it can cause the reader's attention to jump around and miss other parts.

• *Italics*—Not generally used, but if available it can be used in the same manner as underlining in the body of the resume.

• Highlighting—A very new and effective technique. Simply use a translucent color and highlighting pen to dramatize key accomplishments within the body of the resume once it is printed. You can highlight different information for different employers. Best used at lower and middle range positions. A bit too artsy for top management.

• Indenting—Separates different types of information and makes the reader's job easier. Use two or (at most) three different levels as indicated by our samples.

• "Bullets"—These are points of punctuation (• or *) set in front of each item in a list of accomplishments or other results that are short separate points to be made.

FIRST AND SECOND DRAFTS

Don't expect to achieve the best layout styling and impact in your resume on the first draft. Plan to do two or three drafts—either by hand, word processor, or typewriter. Once you have pulled the information together, edit ruthlessly, cutting back sentences that are too long, eliminating redundancies and confusing style.

EDIT AND CRITIQUE

Get the first or second draft critiqued by someone who is very good at grammar, spelling, and punctuation. Don't plan to do this yourself, as most of us have blind spots about our own errors. Please take this critique and editing function very seriously. A surprising percentage of resumes end up getting printed with errors that require redoing at a later date, and cause embarrassment when you discover that you've been sending out imperfect resumes to potential employers.

In having your resume critiqued, make sure the person doing the critiquing knows you want him/her to be as tough as possible and not to make you feel good. Don't present it with the statement or question "Isn't this a good resume?" or "How do you like this?" Rather say, "Do you have any ideas how to make this stronger?" or "Please look for any errors." Thank that person for his/her input.

The critique you want is essentially one that points out errors and lack of clarity. Avoid discussions of format, content, or emphasis unless the person critiquing is really an expert. There is a lot of outdated information floating around in the practices of some counselors and others who have been out of touch with employers' needs. In this book we have presented concepts and examples coming out of our extensive direct experience with job candidates who have been able to get interviews, and out of our involvement in the employment process with hundreds of personnel staff, supervisors, and managers. We may not have all the answers, but we are definitely operating at a pragmatic rather than theoretical level.

On the following page is a checklist of things to look for in critiquing your resume draft.

Resume Critique Checklist

_____ Material fits neatly on one page

_____ No spelling, grammar, or punctuation errors

_____ Typing is neat, clean, and professional looking

_____ Name, address, and telephone numbers are centered at top

_____ Margins at sides and bottom are at least one inch wide

_____ Layout makes reading easy

_____ No paragraphs are longer than ten to twelve lines

_____ Important titles are emphasized by underlining or capital letters where appropriate—and not overdone

_____ Indentions are used to organize information logically

_____ Action words are used to communicate accomplishments and results

_____ Extraneous personal information (height, weight, age, sex, etc.) has been left out

_____ Sentences and paragraphs edited to eliminate unnecessary and redundant information

_____ Overall appearance invites one to read it

_____ Resume demonstrates candidate's ability to produce results

DUPLICATING AND PRINTING

At this point you should have a beautiful, edited, well-typed communication of your skills, abilities, and relevant work history—congratulations for that! You have virtually mastered the process. Time to go to press.

The alternative, especially if you are typing, is to have your resume printed by photo-offset process on a high-quality paper stock by a local printer. In the photo-offset process, a printing plate is prepared right from your original, and the printed copies retain all (or give more) of the snap and crispness of the original. The cost for a hundred copies is minimal—a small investment for a high-class presentation. If you don't know a printer, please check in the yellow pages. Call two or three and get comparative quotes.

Have the printer use a good quality paper stock—not just the routine stuff. White stock is fine, and we feel that it is even better-looking on an ivory, buff, or off-white quality paper—this tends to let the resume stand out against the virtual snowbank of other white letters, resumes, and the other paperwork that clutters most desks.

Why not run it off on your handy photocopy machine? It just isn't good enough, that's why. The image frequently smears, the paper is usually fairly low grade, and the quality isn't consistent. At best, it gets a B–. We're pushing for straight A's.

And that—gentle and persevering readers—is The Perfect Resume. We did it—you and we. By the time you read this, *we've* already done our celebrating and taken our cold shower to pull together the remaining pages in the book. Please treat yourself to a similar acknowledgment when your resume returns from the printer. Toast yourself with the knowledge that you are, in resume terms, better prepared than 95 percent of the job seekers in your ball park.

In Step 6 we'll show you how to put together a cover letter to go with your resume, and starting on page 204 we'll provide some abbreviated job-search techniques.

STEP 6: THE PERFECT COVER LETTER

Despite the clarity and precision of your resume, and the attention to job targets and personal objectives, when all is said and done it remains . . . a printed form. Even with the highest degree of personalization, the resume is seen by most employers as a generalized communication. It remains for them to interpret, analyze, and predict how these very real attributes can be put to work for them in the immediate situation.

Frankly, sometimes employers make the right interpretations, and sometimes they don't. Once you have produced the perfect resume, a customized cover letter is your best way of multiplying the odds of a direct hit right at the center of the employer's interest.

The purpose of the customized cover letter is to communicate a *specific, personalized* message to a *particular* employer, answering the most fundamental employment question of all: *Why should I hire you?*

The cover letter is your way to so distinguish what you have to offer to the target of your choice that the likelihood of an interview is at least doubled.

Given the complexity and uniqueness of today's job market, the cover letter is an increasingly important tool for the high level of career success you seek.

A customized cover letter should go out with each individual resume you send out. Given the aptitude of word processors and software, this step is not as difficult as it might once have been. Simply follow these basic rules.

COVER LETTER RULES

Rule 1—Address it to a Particular Person by Name

Send your letter to the person who can make the hiring decision, by name. Personal letters get read far ahead of form letters. Think of your own experience when you open the mail—the letters addressed to you personally get read first. The form letters to "sir" or "madam" or "occupant" may not be read at all.

Call the firm with which you wish to interview and find out the name (correct spelling, please) and title of the individual in charge of the department you would like to work in. Don't worry if it takes three or four calls. If you get stuck, call the president's office and find out from someone there who is in charge of your area of interest. Don't say that you are looking for a job. Say that you have some information to send and want to make sure it gets into the hands of the right person.

With a little practice you'll find there isn't much problem in ascertaining the names and titles you want. After all, organizations need to maintain contact with their public. Don't make the mistake of aiming too high. Corporate presidents and board chairmen get lots of resumes because their names are so visible. Even with a good cover letter, these are usually "intercepted." Find a person at the department or division level—ideally, the person you would work for if you got the job.

Rule 2—Communicate Something Personal

People who get a lot of mail are wary of form letters and have developed personal techniques to skim quickly before reading to see if, in fact, the letter has a message for them.

In your opening lines, write something that is uniquely associated with the person, division, or organization and that will signal to the reader that you invested the time to communicate personally.

The likelihood of a personal response to your letter is directly related to the degree of personal attention you put into it in the first place. You get what you give.

Some typical "personal" opening lines are:

"I see that you have opened a new shopping mall on the western side of town."

"Dr. Foster in the economics department said that she had talked with you about your expansion plans."

"I understand that you have just received a new study grant from ACW."

Rule 3—Answer the Question "Why Should I See You?"

The work world operates on *value*, not need. You are of interest to a potential employer to the degree that they experience you as being valuable *to them*, not for what you are looking for *from them*.

In the body of your cover letter communicate some special way that your skills will be valuable to the potential employer. Create interest in yourself.

This will take some basic research in your target field and familiarity with the interests and needs of the specific employer, plus a willingness to show how you can make a difference. Common sense helps, as the following examples indicate:

"I feel that my organizational skills could help you in setting up your new customer service department. As you can see from my resume, I have experience in handling service calls in a related field, and could help you train your people."

"My engineering experience with waste disposal in the Red Hook area would be valuable to you in your community landfill project."

"I know that you are aware of the need for publicity and communication with your local community. My work in this area at school, plus my knowledge of the community, will assist you to get the exposure you want."

Take some risks in describing what you feel you can do for this employer. If you are not directly on target, even the fact that you are talking in terms of value rather than need will create interest.

Be careful not to set the letter in a negative tone and criticize or put down what the company has done. Communicate your ability to assist and support not that you threaten what they do.

2301 Meadow Lane
Bull Shoals, AR 72619
January 6, 1989

Dr. Frank Brown
Director of Chemistry
Seville University
Seville, AR 72465

Dear Dr. Brown:

I read your article in *New Science* about "Alternatives to Particulate Pollution." I have done intensive study in this subject and have come up with some theories that might be of value to you.

In addition to discovering a new technique for analyzing particulate content, I have several high-speed designs for simple and inexpensive filter-type mechanisms that can cut particulates up to 85%.

As you will see from the attached resume, I have recently graduated with an M.S. in Chemistry from California Institute of Technology. My master's thesis was "Analytical Methods in Air Pollution," to be published by University Press next fall.

I would like to meet you to further discuss the possibilities of our working together. I will call you shortly to discuss a meeting.

Yours truly,

Jeanne MacGinnis
Jeanne MacGinnis
(801) 396-5555

Rule 4—Use Their Language

Every field has its own jargon and technology. Use the right terms to indicate your ability and expertise. An excellent way to improve your knowledge of the nomenclature of the field is to read trade journals and articles by professionals in that particular field—see your librarian. Watch out for overkill.

2924 Pacific Avenue
San Francisco, CA 94132
April 21, 1989

Mr. James Bell
Executive Vice-President
B.N.B. Finance, Ltd.
550 Pine Street
San Francisco, CA 94108

Dear Mr. Bell:

David Anderson at Bank of America told me about your plans to begin treasury operations here to better serve your Pacific Rim clientele.

Several years ago I created a money market function for a U.S. subsidiary of a Japanese trading company, an experience I think could be valuable to you. I have traded securities for them and performed investment portfolio and other treasury related analysis functions as well.

With my knowledge in these areas, I feel I could be of service to your company in this new operation. I would like to meet with you to discuss some of these ideas further. I will call you next week to arrange a meeting at your convenience.

Yours truly,

Brian Ross

Brian Ross
(415) 253-0822

Rule 5—Ask for the Interview

Salespeople call this the "close"—the time when you ask for the business. In this case the "business" is a personal *meeting* (a more subtle word than interview). Ask for it. You can even suggest a date and time. Here are some closing statements:

"I am planning to schedule interviews at the end of school next month and if possible would like to meet with you during the first week of May. I will call you to set up a date."

"I will be in your area on other business on the 13th of this month and would like to see you then if it's convenient."

---

452 South Rockline Avenue
Seneca, NY 11290
(315) 421-1890

January 23, 1989

Ms. Sandra Breuer
Curator of Impressionist Art
MUSEUM OF MODERN ART
11 West 53rd Street
New York, NY 10020

Dear Ms. Breuer,

I recently read in *Art Forum* that the museum is planning a large Van Gogh exhibit next winter, with the cooperation of Amsterdam's two major museums. I was thrilled to hear that Americans will be able to see these particular masterpieces here for the first time ever.

I have recently graduated from Cornell University. While attending, I had the good fortune to study abroad for one semester. I became very involved with Amsterdam: the people, the sights, but mainly the art. I'm very familiar with the Rijksmuseum, as well as others, and I have an extensive knowledge of their collections.

I feel that my study of Van Gogh's work and the city of Amsterdam and my general background in arts and letters could be of value to you in promoting this exhibit to student groups. I would like to meet with you to discuss some ideas on the subject, and I will call you in a week to ten days to set up a meeting.

Yours truly,

Ken Tyson

Ken Tyson

SPECIAL RESUME NOTES FOR COLLEGE STUDENTS

In the past half-dozen years there has been a major upgrade in the way most schools support students in high-tech job search approaches. Although there are still some reluctant holdouts, most schools have emerged from the era in which students were told to be careful of boasting or taking the initiative with employers, and to let the system work itself out in time-honored ways.

Today's placement center should offer you a comprehensive set of tools to assist in your job search. These will range from a strong reference library of career strategy materials, access to a good employer data base, video interview training materials, a good computerized resume processor, and high-quality laser printing for resumes and cover letters. If this support is not directly available in the career planning or counseling facility, it will often be available at the student center, computer lab, or in some of the school's professional or fraternal societies.

By all means search out—and use—the best resources you can find. It is no longer sufficient to get a degree, stand in line for the campus interviews, and wait for job offers. Today's new graduate has as vast an expanse of work potential for self-fulfillment and financial success as any that have gone before in history.

To capitalize on the enormous potential, however, even with the best tools, you must still exercise your own personal campaign and go for your own personally centered career search. If there are standardized approaches that seem too uniform and conventional and don't allow for you to express your own uniqueness, take your own approaches. Try to avoid standardized, "approved," resume formats that may be most geared to the needs of the school and a large employer body. Express your uniqueness and determination for career excellence in resumes that follow the principles you have learned in this book. If you need to be part of a collegewide career "system," by all means do so. However, remember that this doesn't restrict you from also taking your own initiatives, preparing additional resumes and cover letters, and going beyond the normal. Some tips:

- Consider using the *functional* or *targeted* formats, which don't depend on past experience.

- Stress qualitative factors and leadership roles in campus activities, outside interests, and part-time work.

- Don't be afraid to sound self-assured—even though the tasks you performed seem far removed from a multinational organization.

- Be sure to use spelling checkers, feedback from counselors, and others to help perfect the final versions.

- Use several resumes for several targets.

- Start creating your resume far enough in advance of the employment-interviewing process to ensure time for high quality.

- Use top-quality resume material in summer and part-time job applications.

BOOKING AGENT

JAMES AGEE
291 Russell Avenue
Bridgeport, CT 06606
(203) 733-0859

EDUCATION: B.A., University of Bridgeport   1989

JOB TARGET: BOOKING AGENT

CAPABILITIES:

- Create, develop, and manage jazz and rock groups.
- Develop and implement well-planned budgets and schedules for bands.
- Scout talent for purpose of creating new groups.
- Establish and direct showcase presentations to expose new talent to the public.
- Write press releases and album covers.
- Negotiate fees.

ACCOMPLISHMENTS:

- Promoted five concerts in 2000 seat auditorium for college audiences.
- Created and managed two progressive jazz groups that traveled nine states in 60 days.
- Supervised spring concert series featuring new talent and attended by over 1200 students.
- Wrote numerous reviews on new album releases for college newspapers.
- Booked jazz bands on several campuses and in local clubs.

WORK HISTORY:

1988 - 1989   University of Bridgeport

                    Chairman, Concert Committee

1987 - 1988   The Student Chronicle
                    University of Bridgeport Newspaper

                    Music Critic

1986 - 1987   The Brothers Three/The Music Students

                    Manager/Agent

RESEARCH ASSISTANT

DANIEL M. KARLOFF
309 Berkeley Drive
Syracuse, NY 13210
(315) 492-8711

EDUCATION: B.A., SYRACUSE UNIVERSITY - 1989
Urban Studies

JOB TARGET: RESEARCH ASSISTANT WITH AN
URBAN/REGIONAL PLANNING FIRM

CAPABILITIES:

- Write complete and detailed research reports.
- Edit written materials for content and grammar.
- Work well under pressure to meet deadlines.
- Communicate effectively with librarians and others
  required to support research work.
- Read and summarize detailed or dense material.
- Type reports, memos, and letters on IBM P.C.
- Receive and carry out complicated instructions and tasks.
- Sketch and draw charts and other visual materials
  required to supplement explanatory text.

ACHIEVEMENTS:

- Edited college political magazine and wrote over a dozen
  articles on pertinent and controversial social issues.
- Successfully researched background material for textbook
  on urban economics written by Professor Alfred
  Hinderman.
- Won Senior prize for essay on crime in urban ghettos.
- Maintained A minus average throughout college career.

WORK HISTORY:

1987 - Present   SYRACUSE UNIVERSITY DORMITORY COUNCIL
Newspaper Business Manager
Newspaper Deliverer

1988 - Present   PROFESSOR ALFRED HINDERMAN
Research Assistant

1987 - 1988   SYRACUSE DEMOCRATIC COMMITTEE
Campaign Worker

1986 - 1988   KARLOFF CONSTRUCTION
Laborer

SPORTS WRITER

BOB SAMPSON
11 Randall Avenue
Madison, WI 53715
(608) 433-2981

EDUCATION:

1989	B.A., University of Wisconsin	Journalism

WRITING:

- Wrote 20 articles for the sports section of college newspaper.
- Wrote and sold greeting cards for charity, earning $600.
- Served as assistant editor of the sports section of college newspaper.
- Wrote sports editorials for the final edition of *The Badger News* - school newspaper.

SPORTS:

- Played four years college basketball.
- Nominated "Player of the Year" in state college basketball.
- Coached high school basketball players at summer clinic.
- Responsible for three high school players going on to college with scholarships.

COMMUNICATION / RADIO / VIDEO:

- Announced live broadcasts of football games on college radio.
- Wrote and delivered nightly sports news for radio on football weekends.
- Assisted in developing basketball training via video.
- Delivered sports promotional spots on local college radio station.

WORK HISTORY:

1987 - 1989	BADGER NEWS, University of Wisconsin	Madison, WI
	Assistant Editor/Sports Writer	
1986 - 1987	BADGER RADIO, University of Wisconsin	Madison, WI
	Radio Sports Announcer	
1985 - 1989 Summers	CAYUGA BASKETBALL CLINIC	Green Bay, WI
	Coach and Instructor	

EDITORIAL WRITER

KARLA SALVEN
333 Drexal Drive
Pitman, NJ 08225
(609) 432-0488

EDUCATION: 1989 B.A., JOURNALISM/COMMUNICATIONS
Glassboro State College, Glassboro, New Jersey

WRITING:
- Wrote four full page essays on controversial and political issues for college yearbook.
- Researched and wrote over 50 birth announcements for daily countywide newspaper.
- Reported on local political meetings for daily local paper.
- Reported on pertinent college issues for college newspaper.

EDITING:
- Edited over a dozen newspaper articles on local events.
- Assisted in making all editorial decisions for college yearbook, which won second place in national competition.
- Selected and edited all copy for yearbook.
- Insured accuracy of all information for college freshman general information guide.

MANAGING:
- Selected and hired photographers, and managed the scheduling of all senior class photo sessions.
- Coordinated photographic shootings between five photographers with 143 groups and 203 events.
- Oversaw and approved design and layout of yearbook for two years.
- Coordinated and designed freshman orientation handbook.

PHOTOGRAPHY:
- Shot pictures of local events and groups for daily paper.
- Shot and selected photos for a variety of college publications.

EXPERIENCE:

1985 - 1988	SHADOW, Freshman Orientation Handbook	Editor
	IMAGE, College Yearbook	Assistant Editor
	Glassboro State College	
1986 - 1988	MAINLINE TIMES	Writer/Editor, Local Events
	Vineland, NJ	
1985 - 1986	BORO NEWS	Writer, Announcements
	Glassboro, NJ	

SPECIAL NOTES FOR WOMEN REENTERING THE JOB MARKET

There is strength in numbers. For the most part, in the United States and to a lesser degree in Europe and the rest of the Western World, women no longer need to approach the job arena with the concern for unfair treatment and discrimination that was such a cultural negative in the past. The expanded presence of women in all but the most hardy bastions of male employment supremacy has established itself as one of the most important sociological factors of our time. Career gates have opened, and the flow of qualified women into nontraditional work domains has reached flood tide. Within a few short years it is expected that females will account for nearly two out of three new entrants. With the right tools and personal intention you can truly use your work experience for self-actualization and manifesting your potential. And, of course, the right resume strategies are essential.

Women are still dealing with deeply based, slow to fade cultural pictures of male-dominated workfields (generals, priests, bricklayers, haute cuisine chefs . . .) and the difficulty both employers and sometimes they themselves have to overcome to imagine them in these roles. Aside from this, the single largest difficulty specifically applicable to women is resolving the question of the dual roles of worker and mother/homemaker. How do you explain, express positively, account for, translate, and take advantage of time spent away from the work force in the service of your children, as you reenter the workaday world.

Time spent rearing children, whether two years or fourteen, is a positive choice you made. It does not need to be accounted for as "time away." Many of the home-managing skills and qualities are translatable in your resume to organizational management terminology. Much can also be made of work you have done in community and in semirelated part-time or volunteer work. If you have kept up to date on developments in your field or areas of career interest, including reading periodicals, trade journals, and attending seminars and courses, this can also be highlighted.

If you are planning the next phase of your life to include both home and work, there are an expanding number of options that continue to surface. A growing number of companies support this bilateral focus through part-time, job sharing, flex-time, and even flex-place arrangements.

Computer savvy women may consider "telecommuting"—working from home all or part of the time, linked to an employer by telephone. With modems, networks, and floppy disks it is easy to be "plugged in" to business without leaving your apartment. This is a hot trendline, and if it means that you need to gain some computer expertise by all means do so; the benefits will be great. If the trend continues, by A.D. 2000 up to 20 percent of the work force will be telecommuting at least part of the time.

If you are a woman reentering the job market, focus on the following when creating your perfect resume:

- Experiment with translating the day-to-day of your time away into generic or business related terms. You may think this is all too obvious; however, the big difference shows up in the thinking of an employer who might not think it as obvious as you do.

- Do the same in translating community or volunteer work to commercial terms. *You* might know that the fund-raising drive you ran for your children's school involved: "conducting strategic planning meetings with key team managers, scheduling training and coaching meetings, acquiring professional support systems, implementing innovative telemarketing approaches, and exceeding performance goals by 150%," but your future employers might not—unless you remind them.

- Consider using the targeted or functional resume format, so as to downplay the time away.

- Take enough time to research employer needs in your targeted field. The wider your research and the broader your possibilities, the more you can specifically address the needs of particular employers.

- Compose strong, custom cover letters, with no apologies for your time out to raise children and plenty of good ideas about how you are able to provide valuable results-related service to the employer's needs.

- Emphasize how much you have learned and understand about industry trends and current issues in the field, as well as what you have done that will make a positive contribution. Consider continuing education as well, particularly if you need to develop computer literacy or other special skills.

All experience counts. Much of what you have done at home or school will be applicable to your worklife ambitions. Some won't. Your task in the resume preparation is to actively identify the parts of your life that demonstrate your ability, *and willingness*, to make a contribution. Some pointers:

- Pay particular attention to the Career Discovery Process in the beginning of this book—do the exercises.

- Experiment with the targeted and functional formats and the resume alternative.

- Emphasize the human factors in your career inventory: organizational skills, ability to communicate, supervisory ability, people skills.

- Familiarize yourself with the most current topics in the work world —read trade journals, business publications, books. If you need to, get exposure to actual working environments—through temporary service work, volunteering, and working with friends and relatives who are in business.

- Make a list of twenty friends, professional contacts, ex-professors, neighbors, and relatives who could help you develop additional leads for your resume.

• Stretch yourself—further than you may have thought possible—get rid of any tendencies for self-disparagement or insecurity. In addition to your resume, demonstrate your abilities in the way you dress, the quality of your communication, and your ability to discover opportunities to create value for others.

• Get support in the form of positive reinforcement and honest critique from family and friends. Use all available resources.

See the following cover letter and four sample resumes.

WOMEN REENTERING

200 Avenel Way
Washington, D.C. 20034
April 21, 1989

Mr. Brian Monahan
Associate Director, Office of Mental Health
Community Health Service Board
2333 J Street
Washington, D.C. 20202

Dear Mr. Monahan,

I read the article in last week's *Washington Post*, on the problem of releasing mental patients from facilities without adequate training and preparation for returning to society, with great interest. The article mentioned that your department would be looking at ways to address this issue.

During the past fourteen years, I have had a wide range of experience in creating training material for a number of community and mental health organizations. My experience with nursing home patients, some of whom were mentally ill, might be of particular benefit to you. I am confident that I could help you develop a program that would enable patients who are ready to be released to cope with daily life on their own.

I have given this some thought, and I have several ideas I'd like to discuss with you. I will telephone your office next week to arrange an appointment at your convenience.

Sincerely,

Beverly Rhodes

Beverly Rhodes

PROGRAM DEVELOPER

BEVERLY RHODES
200 Avenel Way
Washington, DC 20034
(202) 791-1774

<u>JOB TARGET</u>:   Program Developer in Mental Health Field

<u>CAPABILITIES</u>:

- Design and develop training material.
- Develop remedial training concepts.
- Write clear and concise proposals.
- Administer and evaluate various skill tests.
- Consult with psychologists and clients.
- Counsel teenagers, troubled and disadvantaged youth.
- Design and deliver oral presentation to large groups.

<u>ACHIEVEMENTS</u>:

- Designed and wrote training manual for the care of isolated patients in nursing homes.
- Created awareness training program for airline personnel to foster better understanding of handicapped passengers' needs.
- Wrote proposal for the training of counselors working with ex-offenders, resulting in $250M federal funding.
- Administered and evaluated tests, including the Wexler and MMPI, to ex-offenders and high school students.
- Developed psychological and skill profiles consulting with psychologist on test results.
- Referred clients to various self-help organizations as a result of testing.
- Counseled 50 teenagers in pregnancy prevention and prenatal care.
- Delivered lectures to various community organizations on the need to support mental health programs.

<u>WORK HISTORY</u>:

1983 - Present	Volunteer with numerous community and mental health organizations.
1982 - 1983	PIEDMONT AIRLINES Consultant in Awareness Training for Handicapped Passengers.

<u>EDUCATION</u>:

1983	GEORGE WASHINGTON UNIVERSITY M.S. in Social Services

LAWYER

SHARON HARTLEY KALEN

340 West End Avenue
New York, NY 10024
(212) 595-4240

EXPERIENCE:

LITIGATION: Attained numerous credits in all phases of civil litigation in state and federal courts. Successfully conducted depositions and trials in a variety of media and commercial cases. Achieved notable results through expertise in state and federal court brief-writing. Reduced costs through self-training and management of department in creditors' rights and bankruptcy cases. Achieved favorable resolution of complex, difficult-to-win cases through meticulous work and deployment of group-supported strategies. Practiced before administrative boards and arbitrators.

MEDIA: Practiced in all aspects of media law for large and medium-sized clients. Conducted and directed media litigations with expertise. Avoided litigation through creative merging of legal and editorial skills in pre-publishing libel and privacy counseling. Analyzed and managed copyright and corporate matters. Planned and negotiated contracts and settlements.

MANAGEMENT: Skilled in perceptive direction of research, planning of trial and pre-trial strategy. Reduced unnecessary time spent by others on work projects through careful supervision of work. Maintained extensive client contact. Selected, supervised, and controlled local counsel in out-of-state cases to assure highest results while avoiding large billings.

EMPLOYMENT HISTORY:

1980 - 1986   BALMER, KAYE, SAAMS & HARTMAN - New York, NY
<u>Senior Associate</u>

EDUCATION:

1980   COLUMBIA LAW SCHOOL - LLB Cum Laude
Harlan Fiske Stone Scholar; Dean's List.

1976   COLUMBIA COLLEGE - B.A. Degree
Top 10% of class; Dean's List.

PUBLICATIONS:

Columbia Journal of Law and Social Problems - Editor
Kings Crown Essays - Managing Editor

DATA PROCESSING

JOAN M. CABRILLO

2280 Bal Harbor Drive
Miami, FL 33154
(305) 274-8096

SUPERVISION: Supervised two IBM 360/30 systems with input/output devices comprising six 2311 disk storage drives, four 240111 tape drives, two 2540 card readers, and two 1403 printers. Exercised full supervisory authority over two supervisors and a staff of 25 computer operators, keypunch operators and control clerks. As supervisor of script stock, directed activities of a staff of 40.

DATA PROCESSING: Formulated mathematical models of systems. Set up controls analog and hybrid computer system to solve scientific and engineering problems. Computed voltage and time scales to convert mathematical equations into computer equations to obtain potentiometer settings.

Drew computer circuit diagrams to indicate connections between components and their values. Observed behavior of variables on output devices such as plotters, recorders, digital voltmeters, oscilloscopes, digital displays, and readouts to obtain solutions.

WORK HISTORY:

1984 - 1987	IBM CORPORATION	Supervisor of Script Stock
1981 - 1984	F.S. SMITH & COMPANY	Operations Dept. Supervisor
1974 - 1981	TROMSON & McKANNON	Supervisor, Computer Room

EDUCATION:

1989	MIAMI DADE COLLEGE	B.S. degree expected Computer Science
1984	UNIVERSITY OF FLORIDA	Programming Design & Analysis
1984	IBM EDUCATION CENTER	

LANGUAGE: COBOL

COUNSELOR

ELLEN SIMPSON
203 Warren Avenue
Spring Lake, NJ 07762
(201) 449-6793

COUNSELING:

- Consulted with parents for probable child abuse and suggested courses of action.

- Partnered with social workers on individual cases in both urban and suburban settings.

- Counseled single parents on appropriate coping behavior.

- Handled pre-intake interviewing of many individual abused children.

TEACHING:

- Instructed large and diverse community groups on issues related to child abuse.

- Taught 30 volunteers to set up community child abuse programs.

- Ran workshops for parents of abused children.

- Instructed public school teachers on signs and symptoms of potential child abuse.

ORGANIZATION/COORDINATION:

- Coordinated transition of children between original and foster homes.

- Served as liaison and child abuse educator between community health agencies and schools.

- Wrote proposal to state for county funds to educate single parents and teachers. Funding accepted.

VOLUNTEER WORK HISTORY:

1983 - 1989   COMMUNITY MENTAL HEALTH CENTER   Freehold, NJ

                  Volunteer Coordinator - Child Abuse Program

1982 - 1983   C.A.R.E. - Child-Abuse-Rescue-Education   Albany Park, NJ

                  County Representative

EDUCATION:

1974   DOUGLASS COLLEGE - New Brunswick, NJ
        B.S., Sociology

Sample Resumes

On the following pages are samples of resumes selected from our files as representing the principles set out in this book. We consider them to be examples of the highest form of the resume-writing art. We have included a variety of occupations as well as types and styles of resumes and levels of experience. Names and addresses have, of course, been changed.

The sample resumes are arranged according to career fields. You will also find a Resume Selector, which gives the resume format as a cross-reference. Identify a field and locate the page alphabetically to review that resume.

If your job target field is not directly represented, don't worry, for many of the resumes in other fields will be of value as a guide. After you have selected the format of your resume, review a number of examples in the same format.

Following the illustrated resumes, we have given a number of examples of job fields not represented by resumes of their own. Much of the basic information in these related paragraphs comes to us courtesy of the *Dictionary of Occupational Titles*.*

The first three resumes are before-and-after examples. Try this: before you look at the "after," see how you would critique the "before," indicating the changes you would make.

*U.S. Department of Labor, Washington, D.C. 1988–89.

THE RESUME SELECTOR

INDEX TO SAMPLE RESUMES

Job Target Field	Sample Paragraph	Chronological	Functional	Targeted	Resume Alternative	Special Interest For College Students	Special Interest For Women Reentering Job Market
Account Executive	192						
Accountant—Recent College Graduate				148		148	
Activities Planner—College	192					192	
Administrative Assistant	192						
Administrative Coordinator					108		
Advertising Media Planner		149					
Art Director	192						
Artist			150				
Assistant Plant Manager (before)			142				
Assistant Plant Manager (after)			143				
Assistant TV Producer (before)			146				
Assistant TV Producer (after)			147			147	
Banker		152					
Biotechnologist	193						
Booking Agent				123			
Buyer, Fashion			153				
Certified Public Accountant	193						
Chemist/Manager			154				
Computer Animator	193						

Job Target Field	Sample Paragraph	Chronological	Functional	Targeted	Resume Alternative	Special Interest For College Students	Special Interest For Women Reentering Job Market
Consultant/Entrepreneur					191		
Copywriter			155				
Corporate Foundation Manager	193						
Corporate Training Manager		73					
Counseling Director	194						
Counselor			134				134
Data Processing—College Graduate			133				133
Dental Hygienist	194						
Design Engineer		159	83				
Die Designer		158					
Drafter	194						
Economist	194						
Editor			156				156
Editorial Assistant	195						
Editorial Writer			126				
Educational Therapist	195						
Electrical Engineer				157			
Employee Benefits Executive				51			
Environmental Health Inspector	195						
Executive Assistant— International		185					
Executive Secretary				160			
Fashion Coordinator	196						
Guidance Director	196						
Guidance Navigation Control Engineer	196						
Hospital Administrator				161			
Human Resources Manager			171				

Job Target Field	Sample Paragraph	Chronological	Functional	Targeted	Resume Alternative	Special Interest For College Students	Special Interest For Women Reentering Job Market
Human Resources–Recent College Graduate		188				188	
Industrial Electronic Equipment Repairer	196						
Internal Auditor	197						
International Investment Banker		183					
Lawyer			132				132
Librarian			163				
Lobbyist	197						
Management Consultant	197						
Management Trainee	197						
Manager, Business			164				
Manager—Chemicals Procurement (before)		144					
Manager—Chemicals Procurement (after)		145					
Manager/Executive		165					
Manager/Insurance			166				
Manager, Retail Store	198						
Manager/Technical				167			
Manufacturing Planner		187					
Market Analyst/Researcher		168					
Marketing Manager	198			169			
Mechanical Engineer	198						
Medical Record Administrator	199						
Merchandise Manager	199						
Nuclear Medicine Technologist	199						
Numerical Control Tool Programmer	199						
Nutritionist			170				
Package Designer	200						

Job Target Field	Sample Paragraph	Chronological	Functional	Targeted	Resume Alternative	Special Interest For College Students	Special Interest For Women Reentering Job Market
Photographer			172				
Plant Engineer	200						
Program Developer		173		131			130
Program Manager		186					
Project Director	200						
Public Relations			174				
Public Relations Representative	201						
Rehabilitative Physiotherapist				175			
Research Assistant		184		124			
Research Nutritionist	201						
Residence Counselor	201						
Retail Management		176					
Robot Technician	202						
Sales, Auto			151				
Sales, Fund Raising			162				162
Sales Manager	202						
Sales/Retail			177				
Secretary		178					
Securities Analyst		179					
Senior Credit Analyst				91			
Social Worker		180					
Sociologist	202						
Sports Writer			125				
Student Affairs Director	202						
Systems Analyst	203						
Teacher				181			
Teacher's Aide	203						
Telecommunications Specialist	203						
Telemarketer			189				

Job Target Field	Sample Paragraph	Chronological	Functional	Targeted	Resume Alternative	Special Interest For College Students	Special Interest For Women Reentering Job Market
Travel Agent		182					
Urban and Regional Planner	203						
Video Engineer			83				
Water and Wastewater Treatment Plant Operator	204						

ASSISTANT PLANT MANAGER

BEFORE

TOM KANDOWSKI
497 Christy St.
Carteret, New Jersey 07008   Telephone 201 546-3876

PERSONAL   Married   6 ft.   190 lb.   27 years old

EDUCATION   Attended Middlesex County College for two years, Majoring in
                    Liberal Arts/Business Administration.

                    Attended Trenton State College, majoring in Political Science.
                    Received Bachelor of Arts degree in December, 1982, with a 3.52
                    cumulative average.

                    Studied Stationary Engineering at Middlesex County Vocational
                    School at night in 1982-83. Received a Blue Seal engineer's license
                    in August, 1983.

                    Studied Basic Machine Shop at Middlesex County Vocational
                    School at night in 1983-85.

SCHOLASTIC   Graduated with Honors from Trenton State College. Dean's list for
ACHIEVEMENTS   four semesters. Was one of the representatives of the Political
                    Science Dept. to the National Model United Nations Conference
                    held in New York in 1981.

WORK   6/76-10/79 Produce and Frozen Foods clerk at Anderson's
EXPERIENCE   Foodtown, 989 Port Reading Ave., Port Reading, N.J., part-time
                    while in school, and full-time during summers.

                    6/80-10/80 Canning Machine Operator at Greater Northeastern
                    Tank Corp. (GNTC), Lafayette St., Carteret, N.J.

                    4/81-7/84 Oiler at Northern Railroad, Port Reading, N.J., for two
                    years. Then promoted to Maintenance Machinist in charge of
                    mechanical work. Duties also included pipefitting and operating
                    steam boilers, engines, lathes, and other machine shop equipment.

                    Worked part-time for several years with a licensed electrical
                    contractor (Lewis Electric Co.), installing residential and industrial
                    services, equipment and wiring.

                    11/84-Present Maintenance Technician at Technicians, Inc. (Data
                    Processing Center), 3678 Park Ave., Metuchen, N.J. Duties
                    included Climate Control and Building Maintenance.

BACKGROUND   Brought up in Carteret area and attended local schools. Delivered
                    Newark Star Ledger newspapers for five years. Member of Carteret
                    High School wrestling team for two years.

INTERESTS   I enjoy reading, fresh-water fishing, camping, music, sports, and
                    traveling.

ASSISTANT PLANT MANAGER

TOM KANDOWSKI
497 Christy Street
Carteret, NJ 07008
(201) 546-3876

AFTER

<u>WORK EXPERIENCE</u>

ADMINISTRATION: Coordinated plant service activities, including installation, maintenance, and repair of equipment for a 30,000-square-foot data processing center. Developed preventive maintenance schedules and handled all follow-through. Maintained perfect OSHA compliance.

MECHANICS: Responsible for repairing and maintaining all mechanical aspects of a railroad coal-dumper, including bearing replacements, pump overhauls, and general machine repairs.

PIPEFITTING: Made extensive steam line alterations and additions following a conversion from coal to #6 oil firing of three boilers totaling 1250 horsepower. Replaced sections of 12-inch boiler headers.

ELECTRICITY: Assisted a licensed electrical contractor in installing residential and industrial services, equipment, and wiring.

STATIONARY
ENGINEERING: Operated and maintained four piston valve steam engines; maintained four slide valve steam engines, and two duplex feedwater pumps. Kept watch on two firetube and one watertube boilers generating 150 psi steam. Responsible for preparing this equipment for insurance inspections.

<u>WORK HISTORY</u>

1984 - Present   TECHNICIANS, INC.   Metuchen, NJ
<u>Maintenance Technician</u>

1981 - 1984   NORTHERN RAILROAD   Port Reading, NJ
<u>Oiler / Maintenance Machinist</u>

1979 - 1981   LEWIS ELECTRIC COMPANY   Port Reading, NJ
<u>Electrician's Assistant</u>

<u>EDUCATION</u>

1983   MIDDLESEX COUNTY VOCATIONAL SCHOOL
Stationary Engineering. Blue-Seal license.

1982   TRENTON STATE COLLEGE
B.A. Degree, with honors.

MANAGER CHEMICALS PROCUREMENT

JOHN HAVLOWE
82 Sherwood Street
Wildwood, New Jersey 07886
(201) 336-9834

BEFORE

BIRTHDATE:	January 18, 1931
HEALTH:	Excellent
HEIGHT:	5' 11"
WEIGHT:	185 lbs.
MARITAL STATUS:	Married, two dependent children

OBJECTIVE: To obtain the position of Purchasing Manager or Director with a company that promotes individual initiative and allows for individual application of Management expertise.

EDUCATION: Upsala College, East Orange, New Jersey
Chemistry and Business

Also 280 hours of various management courses sponsored by Chemicals & Pharmaceuticals, Ltd., and Allied Metals & Alloys Company

EMPLOYMENT:

1975 - Present: <u>Allied Metals & Alloys Company</u>

Corporate Manager - Chemicals Procurement

Responsible for managing a corporate Procurement group which purchases the major chemical raw materials for over 100 consuming plants in the U.S. Commodity responsibility includes pulp and paper chemicals, plastic resins, inks, waxes, coatings, solvents, plastic film and sheet, and lignosulfonates.

1974 - 1975: <u>Allied Metals & Alloys Company</u>

Materials Manager

Designed and implemented necessary systems and procedures to establish purchasing function for M & T Chemicals, a subsidiary of Allied Metals & Alloys. Implemented a cost reduction program resulting in significant savings to the corporation. Coordinated purchasing activities between Corporate Purchasing and M & T Chemicals.

1969 - 1973: <u>Chemicals & Pharmaceuticals, Ltd.</u>

Purchasing Agent

Was responsible for negotiating for approximately $40 million of specialty and commodity raw materials. Contributed significantly to Allied's cost reduction program. Performed liaison function between Corporate Purchasing and Allied of Canada, Ltd. Implemented program to improve reporting systems between plants and Purchasing.

MANAGER CHEMICALS PROCUREMENT

JOHN HAVLOWE
82 Sherwood Street
Wildwood, NJ 07886
(201) 336-9834 (home)
(201) 772-6000 (work)

AFTER

WORK EXPERIENCE:

1974 - Present	ALLIED METALS & ALLOYS COMPANY	Secaucus, NJ

1975 - Present   <u>Manager, Chemicals Procurement</u>

Manage a corporate procurement group that purchases the major chemical raw materials for over 100 consuming plants in the U.S. Commodity responsibility includes pulp and paper chemicals, plastic resins, inks, waxes, coatings, solvents, plastic film and sheet, and lignosulfonates. Direct six professional buyers and non-exempt employees. Designed, developed, and implemented cost reduction programs saving over $1MM per year. Initiated program in support of Hazardous Waste Disposal project. Participated in strategy planning and negotiations for key raw materials.

1974 - 1975   <u>Materials Manager</u>

Designed and implemented necessary systems and procedures to establish purchasing function for M&T Chemicals, subsidiary of AM&A. Coordinated purchasing activities between corporate purchasing and M&T.

1969 - 1974   CHEMICALS & PHARMACEUTICALS, LTD.   Secaucus, NJ

<u>Purchasing Agent</u>

Negotiated for approximately $40MM of specialty and commodity raw materials. Contributed significantly to Allied's cost reduction program. Performed liaison function between corporate purchasing and Allied of Canada, Ltd. Implemented program to improve reporting systems between plants and purchasing.

1964 - 1969   THIOKING CHEMICAL CORPORATION   Union, NJ

<u>Technical Specialist II</u>

Performed research, development, and scale-up on advanced aerospace polymers. Invented seven materials for which patents were awarded.

EDUCATION: Various management courses sponsored by Allied Metals & Alloys and Chemicals & Pharmaceuticals, Ltd.

UPSALA COLLEGE - Lindhurst, New Jersey
Chemistry and Business

ASSISTANT TV PRODUCER
COLLEGE GRADUATE
NO PRIOR PAID WORK EXPERIENCE

```
                         RESUME
                     MARIAN WILSON                        BEFORE

Career Goal:     Entry level position in TV Production


Home Address:    225 Maitland Ave.
                 Teaneck, New Jersey 07666
                 (201) 686-1210

Local Address:   5 Orkney Rd. #4
                 Brighton, Mass. 02146
                 (617) 237-2068

Born:            March 2, 1966
                 Copaigue, New York


Education:       1984-1985:  Elementary Education major at the
                 School of Education, Northeastern University.
                 1987-1988:  Senior at the School of Public
                 Communications, Northeastern University.
                       Major:  Broadcasting and Film
                       Minor:  Sociology

                 High School:  1984 graduate of Teaneck High

1988:            Work at T.V. Graphics, distributing
                 equipment, at Northeastern University's
                 School of Communications.

1988:            Audio Crew for Northeastern University Alumni
                 film.

1987:            School T.V. production presented at public
                 showing.

1986:            Volunteer work for Northeastern University's
                 closed-circuit radio station, WTBU.  Research
                 and on air.

Special Skills:

     Experienced in video equipment including porta-paks,
     studio cameras, mixing and switching boards and slide
     machine.  Experience with audio console including cart
     machine, revox and 350 tape machines.  Experienced in
     Super 8mm cameras, viewers, and splicers.


References furnished upon request.
```

ASSISTANT TV PRODUCER
NO DATES

MARIAN WILSON
225 Maitland Avenue
Teaneck, NJ 07666
(201) 686-1210

AFTER

TELEVISION:

Produced and directed the following video productions: *The Art of Batiking*, *The Impossible Dream*, *The Creative Process*, and *Wildlife Conservation*. Organized all aspects: scriptwriting; audio selection and placement; set design (including furniture building and prop acquisition); lighting design and crew managing; casting; making slides and cue cards; and planning camera shots, angles, and composition.

FILM:

Produced and directed the following: *Everybody Is a Star* and *Love Is a Beautiful Thing*. Handled camera work, editing, splicing, lighting, and soundtrack. Designed and produced all graphics.

RADIO:

Produced a tape demonstrating special effects including echo, reverberations, and speed distortion. Developed a 20-minute documentary: handled interviewing, narration, editing and splicing, and final taping.

TECHNICAL SKILLS:

Operate:
- for TV - studio cameras, porta-paks, handi-cams, and switching panel.
- for film - various super 8mm cameras, viewers, splicers, and 16mm projectors.
- for radio - audio console, turntables, various tape machines, handle cueing, and mixing.

EDUCATION:

1988   NORTHEASTERN UNIVERSITY
         B.S., Broadcasting and Film

1987   F.C.C. - Third Class Operator Permit

ACCOUNTANT
RECENT COLLEGE GRADUATE

JOANNE A. RABAK
820 Westerfield Avenue
Minneapolis, MN 55042
(612) 595-8283

JOB TARGET: ACCOUNTING DEPARTMENT MANAGER

CAPABILITIES:

- Manage large groups of people with ease.
- Analyze vast amounts of data into relevant financial statistics.
- Perform detailed customer audits.
- Develop systems and procedures for all phases of accounting.
- Utilize automated accounting system to produce monthly and yearly financial statements.
- Utilize pc/Lotus and train others.

ACCOMPLISHMENTS:

- Conducted detailed audits of clients.
- Devised specific computer programs for auditing use.
- Supervised daily data input of large accounting department.
- Wrote and researched a detailed study of marketing.
- Administered all trustee-related aspects of bankruptcy proceedings.
- Handled credit analyses and references and made credit recommendations.
- Installed and supervised automated payroll system.

WORK EXPERIENCE:

1986 - Present	KARPSTER & HALBRAND, INC.	Minneapolis, MN
	Staff B Accountant	
1981 - 1984	BARNARD COLLEGE	New York, NY
	Administrative Assistant	
1978 - 1981	OSTERBERG, SHINDLER, & HART, P.C.	New York, NY
	Paraprofessional in Bankruptcy	

EDUCATION:

1988	UNIVERSITY OF MINNESOTA, Graduate School of Business MBA - Accounting
1978	BARNARD COLLEGE B.A. - History

ADVERTISING MEDIA PLANNER

SANDY HARTFORD
425 West 68th Street
New York, NY 10018
(212) 877-9574 - home
(212) 663-0700 - message

1985 - Present	DOBBS, DANE & KRONBACH, INC.	New York, NY

Media Planner

Analyze marketing objectives, formulate media strategies, and recommend best media plans for national computer software/ hardware accounts. Communicate media plans in writing and direct client presentations. Responsible for $6.0 million multimedia account with heavy television as well as $4.0 million heavy print media account. Supervise one assistant planner.

Assistant Media Planner

Tabulated budget, quarterly reports, and spot television recaps and ran comparisons on data-base computer system. Contributed to all media-planning activities such as extensive individual market research on television usage. Participated in strenuous media department training program.

1984 - 1985	KOHENY, SHALLER, & GILBERT, INC.	New York, NY

Media Buyer

Formulated media plans for all direct marketing clients of the agency. Accounts included Fargo's Department Store credit cards. Placed advertisements in major publications and monitored responses.

1982 - 1984	STIX, SCRUGGS & BARNEY, INC.	Chicago, IL

Media Buyer

Negotiated broadcast rates for direct marketing clients. Assisted in traffic, light production of print, casting, and production of radio and television commercials.

EDUCATION:

1982	BRADLEY UNIVERSITY B.S., Advertising	Sterling, IL

ARTIST

Ms. Strong is an artist. She can use strong graphics—she's in the field. She used a combination format since her work history is free-lance and she's had a lot of jobs. Her job target is graphic design.

Katy Strong
145 Fifth Avenue
New York City 10056
h (212) 843-8990/w (212) 345-7880

PASTE-UP/MECHANICALS
GRAPHIC DESIGN

- Produced paste-ups and mechanicals for the weekly "close" of *Newsday* magazine.
- Designed brochures, booklists; selected type, conceptualized and produced monthly silkscreen posters.
- Planned displays for a major metropolitan library.

TECHNICAL ILLUSTRATION
JUNIOR ARTIST/FORMS DESIGNER

- Mastered "LeRoy" lettering technique and created technical illustrations for research publication in the Photo-optics Department at SUNY - Buffalo.

DRAWING BOARD ARTIST/
FREE-LANCE ARTIST/
PHOTOGRAPHER

- Interfaced between client and printer from the drawing board in a commercial printing shop.
- Produced numerous printed materials, from business cards to annual reports.
- Supervised typesetter.
- Supervised a commercial photographic studio.
- Undertook diverse free-lance jobs, including producing a 3' x 5' map of the State University campus, large lettering assignments, portrait and product photography for private individuals, and slide shows for a hospital and the University.

EXPERIENCE:

1984 - Present	Free-Lance Artist
1981 - 1984	STATE UNIVERSITY OF NEW YORK - Buffalo, NY
1985	LEN KOCH, INC. (commercial printing) - Smithtown, NY
1979 - 1981	BUFFALO PUBLIC LIBRARY - Buffalo, NY
1978 - 1979	NEWSDAY, INC. - Chicago, IL

EDUCATION:

1981	THE SCHOOL OF VISUAL ARTS, New York, NY - Commerical/Fine Arts
1978	UNIVERSITY OF CHICAGO - B.A. - General Studies

SALES, AUTO

```
WARREN A. JAMES

517 HEART AVENUE
SEATTLE, WA  98112

(206) 348-0529 - home
(206) 473-1981 - work


AUTOMOBILE SALES/SERVICE:

Handled more than 200 cars over the past 40 years.  Employed
as a mechanic in early career.  Sold personal cars for profit
after extensive use.  Purchased numerous used cars at low
cost and sold them all for profit.  Supervised the
maintenance and repair of 48 vehicles while in the Armed
Services.  During that time, handled truck parts replacement
for 215 Army vehicles of the battalion.


TECHNICAL SERVICES:

Coordinated customer accounts for packing of coffee, nuts,
and bakery products.  Furnished packing information and style
containers necessary for their individual products and
packing procedures.  Had knowledge of customer packing
procedures and was able to reduce material costs for the
company.  Cost savings were in excess of 25% per year.


LABORATORY TECHNICAL SERVICE:

Set up test packs using less costly materials to determine
shelf life.  Supervised group to conduct actual testing
procedures.  Reduced tin coating on cans when tin became
expensive and in short supply through experimentation and
follow-up.


WORK HISTORY:

1957 - Present     ALLIED METAL CORPORATION      Seattle, WA

1969 - Present     Technical Service Representative

1957 - 1969        Laboratory Technician


1957 - Present     AUTOMOBILE SALES/SERVICE (avocation)
```

BANKER

MAHANI L. KATASHEMI
4060 Boulevard East, Apt. 145
West New York, NJ 07190
Home: (201) 863-8542
Office: (212) 792-5360

<u>WORK EXPERIENCE</u>:

1985 - Present   FEDERAL RESERVE BANK OF NEW YORK   New York, NY
<u>Operations Analyst</u>

Responsible for: developing proposals to top management for operational reviews; organizing and managing the task forces to conduct the reviews; documenting and presenting recommendations to top management; coordinating this Bank's efforts with similar initiatives in the Federal Reserve System. Major accomplishments include:

- Initiated, systematized, and managed a review of bank examinations and bank applications processing activities, resulting in annual savings of $1,500,000.

- Developed long-range plan, necessary capital, and operating budgets for the 185-person International Services Department; analyzed costs of foreign exchange and investment transactions.

1983 - 1985   UNITED NATIONS DEVELOPMENT PROGRAM   New York, NY
<u>Planning Officer</u>

Responsible for program planning, resource allocation, and evaluation of a $100 million program of technical and capital assistance to developing countries in the area of population control and economic development. Major accomplishments include:

- Organized and supervised a ten-month, fifteen-person study of the world contraceptive market, sponsored jointly by UNDP and the Ford Foundation.

- Developed a model-based forecasting system for program planning, management, and control.

- Developed population control projects for countries in East Africa and the Middle East.

<u>EDUCATION</u>:

1987   NEW YORK UNIVERSITY, Graduate School of Business
Ph.D., International Banking

1983   MASSACHUSETTS INSTITUTE OF TECHNOLOGY
M.S., Management

1969   RUTGERS UNIVERSITY
B.S., Physics

BUYER, FASHION

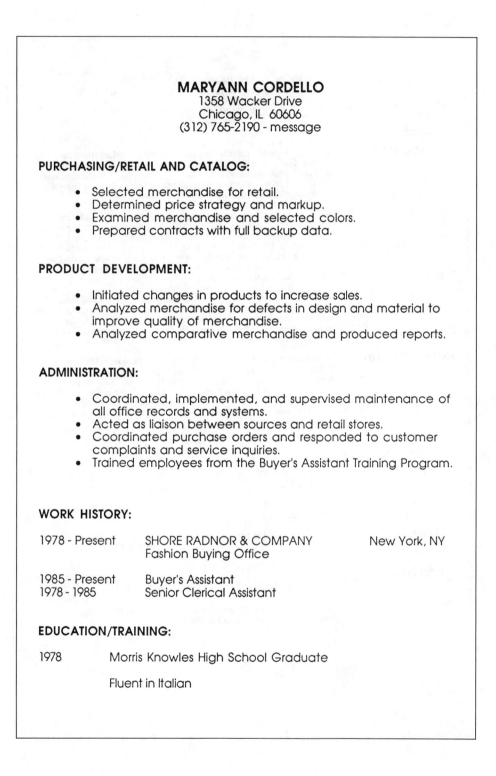

MARYANN CORDELLO
1358 Wacker Drive
Chicago, IL 60606
(312) 765-2190 - message

PURCHASING/RETAIL AND CATALOG:

- Selected merchandise for retail.
- Determined price strategy and markup.
- Examined merchandise and selected colors.
- Prepared contracts with full backup data.

PRODUCT DEVELOPMENT:

- Initiated changes in products to increase sales.
- Analyzed merchandise for defects in design and material to improve quality of merchandise.
- Analyzed comparative merchandise and produced reports.

ADMINISTRATION:

- Coordinated, implemented, and supervised maintenance of all office records and systems.
- Acted as liaison between sources and retail stores.
- Coordinated purchase orders and responded to customer complaints and service inquiries.
- Trained employees from the Buyer's Assistant Training Program.

WORK HISTORY:

1978 - Present	SHORE RADNOR & COMPANY Fashion Buying Office	New York, NY
1985 - Present	Buyer's Assistant	
1978 - 1985	Senior Clerical Assistant	

EDUCATION/TRAINING:

1978	Morris Knowles High School Graduate
	Fluent in Italian

CHEMIST/MANAGER

JOHN C. MORRISON, JR.
34 Candear Street
Tampa, FL 33675
(813) 724-2116

MANAGEMENT: Planned, budgeted, and managed development of products from inception through final production. Hired, developed, and supervised results-oriented professionals and technicians. Organized and coordinated teams of R&D, marketing, and market research people for key projects. Established procedures for managing and controlling projects.

TECHNICAL/ SCIENTIFIC: Achieved technical and consumer objectives for innovative underarm products, facial cleansers, and hand lotions. Solved critical problems in formulating, packaging, and evaluating performance of anhydrous suspension roll-on, pump, aerosol, and squeeze spray deodorants. Supervised manufacture, microbiological safety, and efficacy testing of products. Directed research in dry skin treatment, including developing instrumental methods for evaluating product actions.

Invented processes for surface coloring of gelatin capsules and spray-granulating powders. Developed electronically instrumented tablet presses and an electronic method for measuring antiperspirant activity. Created unique shampoos, rinses, shaving aids, foot sprays, contact lens solutions; plus dentifrice, antiseptic, cold, and vitamin preparations.

COMMUNICATIONS: Maintained R&D liaison with marketing, market research, advertising, legal, and regulatory agencies. Presented key accomplishment and progress reports to senior technical and business management. Handled technical training programs for sales, marketing, and advertising people and prepared comprehensive safety and efficacy manuals to obtain management clearance for sale of products. Interfaced with contract manufacturers, consulting and testing laboratories.

EMPLOYMENT:

1984 - Present   CHEMICAL & METAL PRODUCTS, INC.   Tampa, FL
                  Group Leader

1981 - 1984   JENSEN & JENSEN, INC.   Ft. Lauderdale, FL
                  Group Leader

1965 - 1981   Extensive product and process development experience in various ethical proprietary pharmaceuticals, toiletries, and cosmetic products.

EDUCATION:

ALBANY COLLEGE OF PHARMACY — B.S., Pharmacy

Additional courses in improving managerial skills, pharmaceutical and cosmetic engineering, aerosol technology.

COPYWRITER

MANDY MILES
450 West End Avenue
New York, NY 10023
(212) 787-1993

WRITING/FREE-LANCE:

- Wrote twelve-article series on personal development, fashion, and home furnishings for *Co-Ed* magazine.
- Wrote feature articles for *Ingenue* magazine.
- Created home-sewing shows for *Co-Ed*, given in major department stores nationwide.
- Co-authored paperback book on teenage problems for Pen Publications.

FILMSTRIP PRODUCTION:

- Produced "Loving Relationships" — a half-hour filmstrip for high school students for *Co-Ed*. Wrote "Beautiful Foods" filmstrip for *Co-Ed*.
- Edited over 50 filmstrips for use by high schools in areas of music, art history, and literature for Bramston Publications.

FUND RAISING:

- Assumed major responsibilities in scholarship fund-raising efforts, reaching goals up to $130,000.
- Created craft projects and directed weekly workshops, which produced hundreds of items for large handicrafts bazaar.
- Organized theatrical and cultural benefits, bringing in over $48,000 in three years.

WORK HISTORY:

1979 - Present	Undertook major fund-raising projects and free-lance writing.
1977 - 1979	PARAMETER PUBLICATIONS New York, NY Editor, *Ideas For Youth* — Wrote articles, and supervised art.
1973 - 1977	CO-ED MAGAZINE New York, NY Fashion Editor — Covered fashion markets; supervised photography, art, layout, wrote copy; produced fashion show. Received editorial excellence award from Institute of Men's and Boy's Wear.
EDUCATION:	U.C.L.A. — 1973 — B.A., Art History/English

EDITOR

MARIANNE FURMAN
656 Wyndham Road
Teaneck, NJ 07666
(201) 682-1342

EDITING: Responsible for production editing of social science textbooks for major publisher. Managed complete book production process from copy editing to printing and distribution. Successfully produced over a dozen textbooks.

WRITING: Wrote major best-selling study guides for fiction including Anna Karenina, War and Peace, Don Quixote, and four plays by Ibsen. Wrote introduction and recipes for widely read community cookbook.

RESEARCH: Studied, wrote, published, and widely distributed study materials about the lives and works of Tolstoy, Cervantes, and Ibsen. Developed and shared research techniques that cut participants' study time by 25%.

THERAPY: As psychotherapist, counseled dozens of individuals, couples, families, and groups in mental health centers. Established successful experimental methods based on Viola Spolin's theater games.

EDUCATION: FAIRLEIGH DICKINSON UNIVERSITY - 1988
M.S., Clinical Psychology

ELECTRICAL ENGINEER

```
                        TIM CHOW-CHU

                      792 Ocean Avenue
                     Arlington, VA  22212
                       (703) 883-9763


  JOB TARGET:    ELECTRICAL ENGINEER - Research and Development


  CAPABILITIES:

     *  Conduct R & D concerning design, manufacture, and
        testing of electrical components, equipment, and
        systems.
     *  Apply new uses to equipment.
     *  Design manufacturing, construction, and installation
        procedures.
     *  Direct staff of engineering personnel in producing test
        control equipment.
     *  Direct test programs to insure conformity of equipment
        and systems to customer requirements.
     *  Direct and coordinate field installations.

  ACHIEVEMENTS:

     *  Designed and drafted ship/vessel electrical deck plans
        including power, lighting, and systems and security.
     *  Designed, drafted, and tested telephone relay wirings,
        alarm, and security systems circuitry.
     *  Calculated projects in accord with the latest N.E. Code
        together with the best economic and engineering
        considerations.
     *  Designed and implemented layout of plans, sections and
        details of power distribution, systems, and security.
     *  Designed and implemented layout of H.V.A.C. wirings and
        control wiring diagrams.


  WORK HISTORY:

  1983 - Present  ROSENBLATT, INC.          Washington, DC
                  Junior Electrical Engineer

  1982 - 1983     SMITH-ABBOT, INC.            Arlington, VA
                  Electrical Designer

  1979 - 1982     NATIONAL TELEPHONE         Washington, DC
                  Engineering Aide


  EDUCATION:

  1982            CATHOLIC UNIVERSITY, Washington, DC - B.S., E.E.
```

DIE DESIGNER

FRED M. APRIL
2240 Ponet Drive
Los Angeles, CA 90068
(213) 467-4872

EXPERIENCE:

1983 - Present   MOTOR COACHES, INC.   Santa Monica, CA
                     Die Designer

Responsible for design of small progressive dies to produce ends for metal cans. Participated in design of Button Down and Stay-On Tab ends.

Researched complete end die project for Indonesia, resulting in substantial savings due to prevention of manufacturing redundant and obsolete parts.

Designed tooling for manufacture of plastic tops for Dixie Cup Division.

1981 - 1983   WATSON-EDISON COMPANY   Pacific Palisades, CA
                  Designer

Designed conveyor layout for plant. Designed structural platforms and rings, floor layout for installation of presses, hoppers, and other heavy equipment. Designed carbon-air batteries for use on railroads and buoys. Designed small fixtures to speed up and ease assembly line production.

1980 - 1981   MOTOR COACHES, INC.   Santa Monica, CA
                  Design Draftsman

Designed can-closing machine hookups to fillers; layout work on presses and dies. Designed open end detector used on can-closing machines to detect incomplete curled end seams after cans are sealed.

1971 - 1980   YARDLEY ELECTRIC CORPORATION   Los Angeles, CA
                  Designer

Designed three silver-cell batteries for use in aerospace systems. Participated in the design of the "Hamilton Standard" battery used in the backpack of astronauts to maintain temperature in space suit.

Illustrated technical materials and posters, most notably 30" x 40" color renderings of two Air-Zinc batteries designed for the U.S. Army Signal Corps. Also handled cover illustrations for the company pamphlet distributed at the I.R.E. show.

EDUCATION:

1972 - 1973   LOS ANGELES COMMUNITY COLLEGE
1970 - 1972   DELEHANTY DRAFTING INSTITUTE
1962 - 1964   U.C.L.A.

DESIGN ENGINEER

JIM PEDUSKY
31 Lookout Street
Cranford, NJ 07405
(201) 838-9084

EXPERIENCE

1978 - 1989   INDUSTRIAL METAL COMPANY   Cranford, NJ

1980 - 1989   Design Engineer

Contributed significantly to the design and development of the firm's metal products. Put prototype products into commercial production, maintaining a budget and meeting deadlines. Designed and developed high-speed transfer presses, roll-forming machinery, assembly machinery, and associated tooling, gauges, feed mechanisms, and controls.

Led designers, detailers, and machine shop personnel on major projects dealing with both customers and vendors.

Member of the engineering center "Computer Use Committee." Responsible for the choice and research of new programming.

1978 - 1980   Mechanical Technician

Debugged and modified new equipment. Successfully directed efforts to the development of new metal products.

1976 - 1978   L & R MECHANICAL LABORATORY   Wayne, NJ

Machinist and Toolmaker

Performed all facets in the making of precision tools and gages. Experienced the programming and setup of numerical control machines.

1974 - 1976   BOWLES ENGINEERING COMPANY   Paramus, NJ

Machinist

Performed basic machining on many types of components and machines.

EDUCATION

1985 - Present   FAIRLEIGH DICKINSON UNIVERSITY
110 credits with high academic standing (3.82 out of possible 4.0).

EXECUTIVE SECRETARY

DEBORAH K. MAXELL
220 West E Street
Washington, D.C. 20009
(202) 998-7236

JOB TARGET: EXECUTIVE SECRETARY TO PRESIDENT

CAPABILITIES:

- Create and maintain a simple, highly workable file system.
- Supervise office staff with diverse duties.
- Handle high-pressure situations and deadlines.
- Compose and prepare routine correspondence.
- Prepare financial and other reports.
- Handle purchasing for large office.
- Handle travel and hotel arrangements.
- Manage social as well as business correspondence.
- Handle accounting procedures on IBM or Macintosh.

ACHIEVEMENTS:

- Maintained business relationships with high-level financial executives.
- Supervised staff including assistant, receptionist, steward, and wire operator.
- Assisted with daily cash reconciliation.
- Planned itineraries; arranged trips.
- Assisted editing of financial reports.
- Maintained business and personal calendars.
- Took and accurately transcribed dictation.
- Arranged installation of electronic quotation equipment for 100 branch offices.
- Handled documentation to facilitate international banking arrangements for firm's officers.

WORK HISTORY:

1985 - Present	AZOR CORPORATION Executive Secretary to Vice President of Finance	Arlington, VA
1984 - 1985	GENERAL SECURITIES CORPORATION Executive/Personal Secretary to Vice President	Washington, DC
1977 - 1984	JASON-WALKER, INC. Executive Secretary to Executive Vice President	Washington, DC

EDUCATION: S.U.N.Y. Buffalo
BENTLEY BUSINESS SYSTEMS
NEW YORK INSTITUTE OF FINANCE

HOSPITAL ADMINISTRATOR

NED FILLO
14 Rosewood Lane
Garden City, NY 11530
(516) 737-7280

JOB TARGET: HOSPITAL ADMINISTRATOR

CAPABILITIES:

* Handle in-depth coordinating and planning.
* Direct complex activities in operations and finance.
* Contribute to hospitals, health care facilities, HIP, Fortune 500 industrial, and commercial operations.
* Manage commercial medical administration for headquarters as well as divisions.
* Act as liaison among diverse groups.
* Establish and maintain excellent budget reports.

ACHIEVEMENTS:

* Developed and implemented policies and procedures for eight medical centers serving 125,000 HIP subscribers.
* Recruited and hired administrative staff for eight centers.
* Assisted Chief Administrator in training program preparation.
* Prepared and maintained capital project status and budget reports for New York City's 18 hospitals and care centers.
* Communicated directly with Executive Directors.
* Acted as liaison officer with contractors, vendors, and department heads, interrelating with medical staff regarding their needs.
* Coordinated multi-shop activities for a major health care complex.
* Established an on-site office for a major missile producer.
* Recruited, trained, and directed employees responsible for stocking missile site with capital equipment spare parts.

WORK EXPERIENCE:

1984 - Present	PAN BOROUGH HOSPITAL CENTER	Maintenance Control Planner
1981 - 1984	LA JUANIA MEDICAL GROUP	Administrative Coordinator
1980 - 1981	NEW YORK CITY HOSPITALS CORP.	Planning Analyst
1979 - 1980	NEW YORK UNIVERSITY HOSPITAL	Ad. Asst. - Director of Engineering
1962 - 1979	Project Planner on various corporate government contracts	

EDUCATION:

1960	COLUMBIA UNIVERSITY M.S. in Public Health

SALES/FUND RAISING

MAUREEN ARNOLD
242 North End Drive
Bethel, KY 05394
(217) 643-0972

SALES/FUND RAISING:

* Sold Avon Products to over 500 private clients, grossing $36,000 in sales in one year.
* Raised over $700,000 for the American Heart Association through a Bike-a-Thon.
* Increased Saturday sales in women's clothing boutique by 30% in six months.

MANAGING:

* Managed small boutique in owner/manager's absence.
* Planned and coordinated all details in producing Bike-a-Thon.
* Oversaw promotional activities for Bike-a-Thon.
* Managed all planning and administration for Cub Scout outings.

SUPERVISING:

* Supervised a staff of five volunteers for the American Heart Association.
* Supervised all activities of ten Cub Scouts for two years.
* Managed group of 75 Cub Scouts and seven volunteer adults on weekend district-wide camping trip.

EXPERIENCE:

1986 - Present	ANNIE PINK'S BOUTIQUE Sales - Part-time
1982 - 1988	AVON Sales Representative
1980 - 1981	AMERICAN HEART ASSOCIATION Manager of Bike-a-Thon
1979 - 1981	BOY SCOUTS OF AMERICA Den Mother - Troop 405

EDUCATION:

1987	BETHEL COMMUNITY COLLEGE - Bethel, KY Courses in Business Management

---

LIBRARIAN

Alicia Sherman
170-72 Melbourne Street
Jackson Heights, NY 11328
212-791-8037

LIBRARY CONSULTING

Revised and edited author catalogue. Verified entries in bibliographic sources. Set up outreach program that resulted in 30% greater use of library. Conducted senior citizens seminars that included extensive use of audiovisual materials. Handled book selection and ordering. Processed gift books and film programming. Developed and administered high school English language library.

LIBRARY RESEARCH & REFERENCE

Handled extensive reference work in social and behavioral sciences. Trained numerous small groups in use of reference sources such as card or book catalogue or book and periodical indexes to locate information. Demonstrated procedures for searching catalogue files. Serviced government documents. Maintained vertical and curriculum files as well as film programs and book reviewing.

WORK EXPERIENCE:

1988   AMERICAN MUSEUM OF ANCIENT HISTORY LIBRARY, Consultant

1982 - 1987   QUEENSBOROUGH PUBLIC LIBRARY, Flushing Branch Librarian

PUBLICATIONS:

Author Catalogue; American Museum of Ancient History for their library. Jewish Americans and their History: Sources, American Library Association.

AFFILIATIONS:

American Library Association

EDUCATION:

QUEENS COLLEGE

1984   Masters in Library Science
1981   B.A. in History

MANAGER, BUSINESS

ROBERT C. WHITE
87 South Columbia Avenue
White Plains, NY 10604
(914) 883-8052

MANAGEMENT:

- Hired telephone consultant engineers, training them in technical and interpersonal communications.
- Successfully expanded this group from three to fifteen.
- Developed career path strategy and created charts with management for levels ranging from telephone consultant to project engineer.

TRAINING:

- Trained over 150 people, over ten months, including senior executives, critical care area managers, salesmen, and field engineers.
- Established task analysis and course objectives for these trainees.
- Applied critical judgement and professional competence in instructing over 85 field personnel in various locations.

ADMINISTRATION:

- Handled inventory of technical education department.
- Organized information for budget and delivered to management.
- Supervised small group responsible for maintaining logistics for telephone central operations.
- Developed telephone call sheet formats that were later computerized, resulting in failure analysis reports now used nationwide.

TECHNICAL:

- Responsible for instruction on mini and micro computer-controlled biomedical instrumentation.
- Developed troubleshooting procedures and charts on assigned instrumentation for customer and field service manuals.
- Served as national technical backup to service engineers on existing and developmental instrumentation.
- Performed the operational maintenance, troubleshooting, repair, retrofit, and updating of in-house production and customer education instrumentation.
- Served as quality control inspector for repair group under my supervision.

1982 - Present   TECHNICAL PRODUCTS CORPORATION   White Plains, NY

                       Technical Instructor

EDUCATION

Current   WESTCHESTER COMMUNITY COLLEGE - Electrical
                   Engineering
1982   Technician Certificate
1979   Electronics Certificate

MANAGER/EXECUTIVE

MARCIA S. LOHMAN

421 East Haley Street
Philadelphia, PA 19146
(215) 234-7988

1983 - Present   IMPETUS   Philadelphia, PA

<u>Executive Vice President, Programs for Employers</u>

Managed all administrative operations. Directed the
work of five functional units. Active in formulation
and implementation of organizational policy.
Planned, developed, and evaluated programs and
publications. Developed and designed programs and
materials. Prepared brochures and other
promotional material to increase sales.

1976 - 1983   NATIONAL RESEARCH &
DEVELOPMENT CORPORATION   Philadelphia, PA

<u>Corporate Director of Operations</u>

Managed all educational and manpower projects.
Assisted project directors in all technical
management functions. Prepared proposals for both
private and public funding sources. Negotiated
contracts. Evaluated on-site operations to insure
effective implementation of contractual
requirements.

1975 - 1976   OFFICE OF ECONOMICS - CITY OF NEW YORK

<u>Director of Research, Office of Inspection</u>

Organized and maintained an "early warning system"
to identify local community action problems for
agency director. Coordinated national inspection
visits. Prepared research reports for the agency's
Congressional presentation.

1970 - 1975   Various research positions in New York City.

EDUCATION:

1969   MIAMI UNIVERSITY - Oxford, OH
B.A. - Honors in English

MANAGER, INSURANCE

ROBERT M. BRADLEY
72 Meadows Road
Southfield, MI 48037
(313) 279-8809

MANAGER:

MANAGEMENT:

Responsible for day-to-day smooth operation of home office. Hired and trained personnel in selling insurance and processing claims. Reviewed activity reports for status of sales quotas, underwriting and crediting collections to accounts. Developed sales methods leading to 60% sales increase in nine months. Reconciled commission accounts for salespersons.

SALES:

Sold insurance to 20 new major accounts in six months. Sold increased insurance to over 12 present customers. Analyzed insurance requirements for over 100 prospective clients. Supervised ten salespersons; trained them in sales techniques resulting in a 60% increase in sales.

UNDERWRITING:

Processed risks ranging from small $5,000 single engine aircraft to large multi-engine $30 million commercial jets. Increased territorial premium volume by 20%. Revised underwriting manual; developed new claims forms; set up underwriting training program.

WORK HISTORY:

1983 - Present   AERONAUTICS UNDERWRITERS, Southfield, MI

1987 - Present	Manager of Office Services
1985 - 1987	Underwriter
1984 - 1985	Assistant Underwriter
1983 - 1984	Special Agent

1977 - 1983   U.S. AIR FORCE

Pilot/Operations Officer/Squadron Commander

EDUCATION:

1978	COLLEGE OF INSURANCE
1977	STEVENS INSTITUTE OF TECHNOLOGY

MANAGER/TECHNICAL

WARD GANTNEY
250 Fort Salonga Road
Northport, NY 11687
(516) 725-5286

JOB TARGET: MANAGEMENT - MATERIALS SCIENCE, INSTRUMENT
APPLICATIONS OR SALES

CAPABILITIES:

- Write, edit, and approve professional reports.
- Provide consultation to U.S. Government on contamination problems.
- Set up procedures and special techniques for the nondestructive analysis of integrated circuits, printed circuit boards, semiconductor devices, laser materials, and inertial components.
- Organize and maintain analytical facilities for the characterization of metals, alloys, ceramics, polymers, plastics, fluids, and lubricants.
- Manage programs in materials and component development.
- Conduct corrosion and outgassing studies.

ACHIEVEMENTS:

- Supervised analytical chemistry lab of six to nine graduate chemists.
- Acted as troubleshooter for equipment failure associated with aerospace and ocean systems.
- Purchased all technical equipment.
- Set up nondestructive testing procedures for failure analysis of integrated circuits.
- Conducted comparative analysis of surfactants in electroplated and anodized parts.
- Assisted in developing procedure for removing carbon inclusions from diamonds.

WORK HISTORY:

1961 - Present	GAGE-WEST CORPORATION Supervisor, Analytical Chemistry Lab	Garden City, NY
1985 - 1986	DARNELL ELECTRONICS Consultant	Bethpage, NY
1984 - 1986	R.E.T. SURFACE CHEMICALS Consultant	Northport, NY

EDUCATION:

1976	LONG ISLAND UNIVERSITY Business Administration
1962	HOFSTRA UNIVERSITY B.A., Chemistry; M.A., Microbiology/Oceanography

MARKET ANALYST/RESEARCHER

ROBERT M. GORMAN, C.F.A.
53 Rutgers Drive
Port Washington, NY 11050
(516) 882-5082

1978 - Present	W.B. WHITNEY & COMPANY	New York, NY

Electrical/Electronic Analyst

Follow the major appliance, consumer electronic, and electronic
component industries. Analyze companies and industries and
evaluate stocks. Handle numerous clients such as banks mutual
funds, and insurance companies. Discuss findings, predict market
trends, and advise clients on sensitive issues.

1972 - 1978	I.M.C. DIVISION OF M.R.W., INC.	Philadelphia, PA

Market Research Manager

Supervised two analysts in performing studies on the market for
fixed and variable resistors in the television, computer, automotive,
and other electronic markets. Forecasted potential acquisitions.
Chaired the Electronic Industries' Association Resistor Marketing
Committee.

1968 - 1972	WOLMITE CORPORATION	Waltham, MA
	Transistor Division	

1970 - 1972   Market Research Manager

Identified applications and markets of various semiconductor
technologies. Evaluated potential markets and monitored trends in
the computer, power rectifier, television, automotive, and
instrumentation markets.

1968 - 1970   Senior Engineer

Designed high-current rectifier test equipment and trained customers
on rectifier applications.

EDUCATION: WESLEYAN UNIVERSITY - M.A., Electrical Engineering
NORTHEASTERN UNIVERSITY - B.S.

MARKETING MANAGER

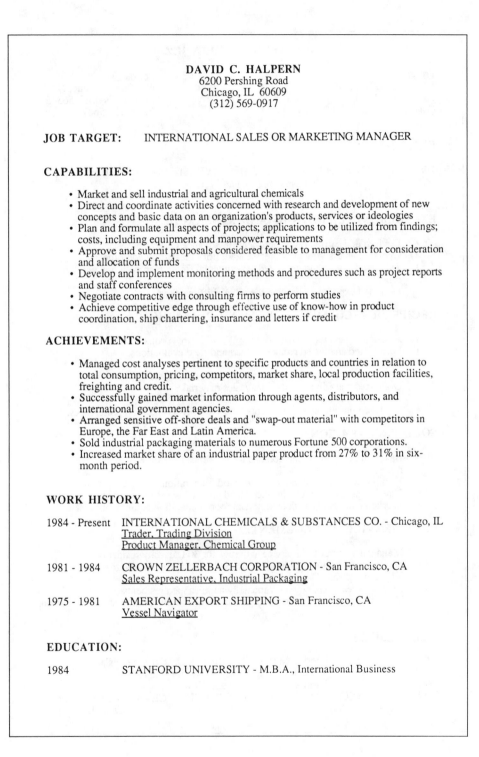

DAVID C. HALPERN
6200 Pershing Road
Chicago, IL 60609
(312) 569-0917

JOB TARGET: INTERNATIONAL SALES OR MARKETING MANAGER

CAPABILITIES:

- Market and sell industrial and agricultural chemicals
- Direct and coordinate activities concerned with research and development of new concepts and basic data on an organization's products, services or ideologies
- Plan and formulate all aspects of projects; applications to be utilized from findings; costs, including equipment and manpower requirements
- Approve and submit proposals considered feasible to management for consideration and allocation of funds
- Develop and implement monitoring methods and procedures such as project reports and staff conferences
- Negotiate contracts with consulting firms to perform studies
- Achieve competitive edge through effective use of know-how in product coordination, ship chartering, insurance and letters if credit

ACHIEVEMENTS:

- Managed cost analyses pertinent to specific products and countries in relation to total consumption, pricing, competitors, market share, local production facilities, freighting and credit.
- Successfully gained market information through agents, distributors, and international government agencies.
- Arranged sensitive off-shore deals and "swap-out material" with competitors in Europe, the Far East and Latin America.
- Sold industrial packaging materials to numerous Fortune 500 corporations.
- Increased market share of an industrial paper product from 27% to 31% in six-month period.

WORK HISTORY:

1984 - Present   INTERNATIONAL CHEMICALS & SUBSTANCES CO. - Chicago, IL
Trader, Trading Division
Product Manager, Chemical Group

1981 - 1984   CROWN ZELLERBACH CORPORATION - San Francisco, CA
Sales Representative, Industrial Packaging

1975 - 1981   AMERICAN EXPORT SHIPPING - San Francisco, CA
Vessel Navigator

EDUCATION:

1984   STANFORD UNIVERSITY - M.B.A., International Business

NUTRITIONIST

ALICE KASIELWICZ

Present:
123 Burgum Hall, NDSU
Fargo, ND 58105
(701) 237-8329, or 241-2073

Permanent:
405 First Avenue, N.W.
Little Falls, MN 56345
(612) 632-5687

EDUCATION:

1989   NORTH DAKOTA STATE UNIVERSITY — B.S. degree
         Major: Administrative Dietetics

EXPERIMENTAL METHODS AND RESEARCH:

- Devised and carried out experiments in advanced food classes.
- Operated an assortment of precise laboratory measuring equipment.
- Tabulated results and presented experimental findings in both oral and written reports.
- Designed experiment varying the oil in chiffon cakes.

RECIPE DEVELOPMENT AND MENU PLANNING:

- Assisted in developing the Cooking With Pictures project.
- Formulated and tested recipes in class and field evaluations.
- Critiqued and evaluated a variety of recipes.
- Assisted in creating the layouts and printing of recipes.
- Organized and edited promotional/sales material.
- Developed menus and market orders.
- Analyzed nutritional requirements for all age levels and food preferences.

FOOD PREPARATION:

- Baked breads, cakes, and cookies for hundreds of people (with and without mixes).
- Familiar with all basic principles of food preparation.
- Have prepared complete, balanced, and appetizing meals in quantities.
- Worked extensively with commercial food preparation equipment.

FOOD SERVICE MANAGEMENT:

- Managed summer food service activities for 30 fraternity residents.
- Supervised all aspects of food service for a special weekend project during NDSU's Upward Bound program.
- Directed meal preparation for mentally handicapped residents.
- Took charge of all summer food procurement and preparation at Camp Watson.

EMPLOYMENT:

1986 - 1989	NDSU - Food & Nutrition Department, Dr. Bettie Stanislao
1987	NDSU - Resident Dining Center, Auxiliary Enterprises
1987	NDSU - Farmhouse Fraternity and Upward Bound
1986	CHILDREN'S VILLAGE FAMILY SERVICE - Mr. Vern Lindsay, Camp Director

HUMAN RESOURCES MANAGER

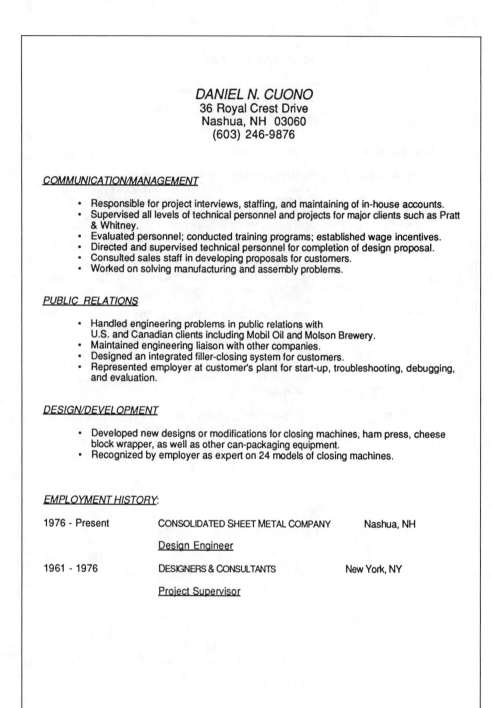

DANIEL N. CUONO
36 Royal Crest Drive
Nashua, NH 03060
(603) 246-9876

COMMUNICATION/MANAGEMENT

- Responsible for project interviews, staffing, and maintaining of in-house accounts.
- Supervised all levels of technical personnel and projects for major clients such as Pratt & Whitney.
- Evaluated personnel; conducted training programs; established wage incentives.
- Directed and supervised technical personnel for completion of design proposal.
- Consulted sales staff in developing proposals for customers.
- Worked on solving manufacturing and assembly problems.

PUBLIC RELATIONS

- Handled engineering problems in public relations with U.S. and Canadian clients including Mobil Oil and Molson Brewery.
- Maintained engineering liaison with other companies.
- Designed an integrated filler-closing system for customers.
- Represented employer at customer's plant for start-up, troubleshooting, debugging, and evaluation.

DESIGN/DEVELOPMENT

- Developed new designs or modifications for closing machines, ham press, cheese block wrapper, as well as other can-packaging equipment.
- Recognized by employer as expert on 24 models of closing machines.

EMPLOYMENT HISTORY:

1976 - Present	CONSOLIDATED SHEET METAL COMPANY	Nashua, NH
	Design Engineer	
1961 - 1976	DESIGNERS & CONSULTANTS	New York, NY
	Project Supervisor	

PHOTOGRAPHER

MARGARET SAWHILL

106 West University Parkway
Baltimore, MD 21210
(301) 655-3178

MAJOR WORK EXPERIENCE:

Photography: As staff photographer for magazine, designed setups for and photographed food products. Covered trade convention personnel and equipment. Photographed restaurant interiors and institutional equipment. Illustrated articles on interior decoration. Shot outdoor scenics and nature close-ups. Photographed "how-to" series on construction projects, food preparation, and maintenance. Taught basic photography to salesmen.

Writing: Researched and wrote scientific articles in fields of chemistry, mathematics, and physics. Converted scientific data into lay terms. Researched and developed articles on industrial equipment, plastics, and food service. Wrote instruction manuals on data processing procedures.

Editing: Edited technical and semi-technical manuscripts in science field. Solicited authors for technical articles. Edited trade magazine copy. Made layouts and dummied pages. Free-lance edited science books.

EMPLOYERS:

1986 - 1989   GARBIER, INC.   Miami, FL
               Executive Assistant

1980 - 1986   EDIFICE MAGAZINE   Baltimore, MD
               Staff Photographer/Assistant Editor

1979 - 1980   MIAMI ACADEMY OF SCIENCES   Miami, FL
               Associate Editor

EDUCATION: MARYLAND INSTITUTE OF ART
               Non-credit courses in painting

               MIAMI UNIVERSITY
               B.A. Degree

PROGRAM DEVELOPER

AGATHA WHITEHEAD
6450 Lindell Boulevard
St. Louis, MO 63110
(314) 752-3438

JOB TARGET: CONFERENCE AND SEMINAR MANAGEMENT

1985 - Present   WASHINGTON UNIVERSITY, School of Continuing Education   St. Louis, MO
Director of Program Development

Designed and staffed 40 programs focused on business and career development. Redesigned the career program to include: personnel management, basic and advanced career workshops, arts management, communication skills for secretaries, fund raising and grantsmanship, and fundamentals of marketing.

Managerial and administrative responsibilities include: Course conceptualization and design, faculty hiring and salary negotiation, administrative staff supervision, public relations, location selection, and space negotiation.

1983 - 1985   WNAL-FM RADIO STATION   Clayton, MO
Program Producer/Host

Originated VOICES, a weekly radio show focused on human development and public affairs. Topics include: career and life planning, women and management, EEO, Title IX, book and film discussion and reviews, job satisfaction, adult life stages, and the quality of work life.

Production and administrative responsibilities included: research of topics, development of discussion formats, selection and scheduling of guests, promotion on air and off, and interviewing.

1979 - 1983   CLAYTON CENTRAL SCHOOL DISTRICT   Clayton, MO
Humanities Instructor

Improved student performance and teacher accountability. Developed and implemented innovative learning contracts incorporating needs assessment, performance objectives, and joint student/teacher evaluation procedures.

Trained staff in individualized learning methods. Organized and coordinated a symposium of Futuristics and a community Ethnic Festival now held every year. Improved communications as a liaison among schools, Humanities Departments, and communities via direct mail, large and small group presentations, and audio-visual programs on various topics.

EDUCATION:

1979   ST. LOUIS UNIVERSITY
B.A. degree; M.A. in progress

PUBLIC RELATIONS

WILLIAM J. WILLIAMS
84 Westfield Road
Richmond, VA 23203
(804) 988-7709

PUBLIC RELATIONS: Handled customer complaints in large retail store. Organized employee/customer liaison group and represented employee views to management. Conducted interviews with prominent sports figures for publication in local paper. Successfully negotiated language and living relationships in Switzerland. Acted as spokesperson for college track team.

SALES: Sold merchandise in nationally known department store. Handled three times previous volume in sales. Produced high sales of six previously slow-moving items. Trained three other successful salespersons.

ACCOUNTING: Handled all bookkeeping and accounting for local retail store. Initiated and implemented computer-based payroll system and created financial reports. Supervised all purchases, reducing incidental expenses by 30%.

EXPERIENCE:

1986 - Present	MADE IN AMERICA STORES Bookkeeper	Richmond, VA
1983 - 1986	K-MART Salesperson	Richmond, VA
1981	CIBA-GEIGY CORPORATION Shipping Clerk	Richmond, VA

EDUCATION:

1986	UNIVERSITY OF VIRGINIA B.A., English	

SPECIALTIES: Have lived nine months in Switzerland.
Proficient in reading, writing, and speaking French.

REHABILITATIVE PHYSIOTHERAPIST

JACKSON F. GARDNER
7142 Hickory Drive
Seville, CO 81009
(303) 249-7269

JOB TARGET: REHABILITATIVE PHYSIOTHERAPIST

ABILITIES:
- Determine appropriate treatment for muscular injuries.
- Accurately diagnose sprains, strains, and ruptures.
- Prepare detailed home-care programs.
- Train loss-of-limb patients in use and care of prosthetic devices.
- Instill motivation in newly handicapped patients.
- Train medical personnel in basics of physical therapy.
- Accurately evaluate physician's recommendations.
- Administer therapy by light, heat, water, and electricity.
- Effectively use ultrasound and diathermy equipment.

ACCOMPLISHMENTS:
- Diagnosed and treated hundreds of patients successfully.
- Performed extensive patient tests and evaluations such as range of motion, functional analyses, and body parts measurements.
- Administered a variety of massage techniques, deep and superficial.
- Administered traction equipment to patients.
- Prepared accurate records of patient treatment and progress.
- Fitted patients with orthotics.
- Trained patients in manual therapeutic exercises for home care.
- Assisted patients in adjusting daily activities to support their condition.

WORK HISTORY:

1985 - Present
ST. MARY'S HOSPITAL
Seville, CO

Colorado Staff Physical Therapist

1985
UNIVERSITY OF MICHIGAN MEDICAL CENTER
Ann Arbor, MI

Intern Physical Therapist

EDUCATION:

1985
UNIVERSITY OF MICHIGAN
B.S., Physical Therapy

1985
Certificate of Physical Therapy

RETAIL MANAGEMENT

Robert's job allows him to be more adventurous in use of typesetting.

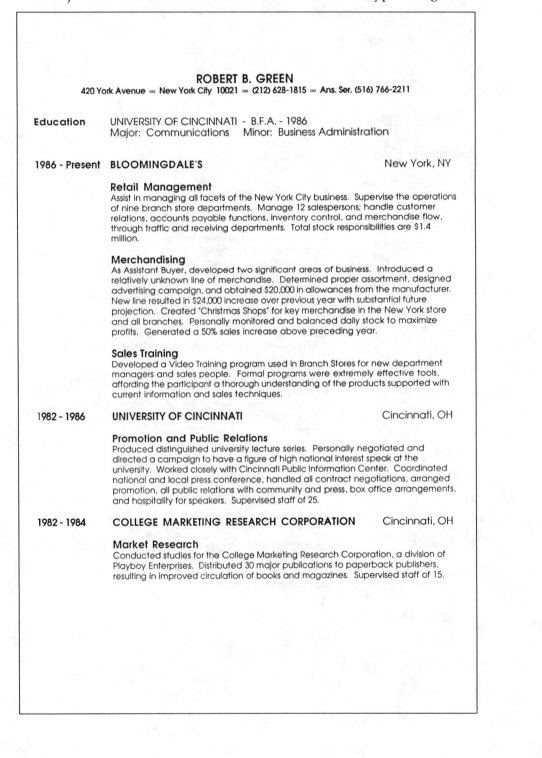

ROBERT B. GREEN
420 York Avenue ∞ New York City 10021 ∞ (212) 628-1815 ∞ Ans. Ser. (516) 766-2211

Education   UNIVERSITY OF CINCINNATI - B.F.A. - 1986
Major: Communications   Minor: Business Administration

1986 - Present   BLOOMINGDALE'S   New York, NY

Retail Management
Assist in managing all facets of the New York City business. Supervise the operations
of nine branch store departments. Manage 12 salespersons; handle customer
relations, accounts payable functions, inventory control, and merchandise flow,
through traffic and receiving departments. Total stock responsibilities are $1.4
million.

Merchandising
As Assistant Buyer, developed two significant areas of business. Introduced a
relatively unknown line of merchandise. Determined proper assortment, designed
advertising campaign, and obtained $20,000 in allowances from the manufacturer.
New line resulted in $24,000 increase over previous year with substantial future
projection. Created "Christmas Shops" for key merchandise in the New York store
and all branches. Personally monitored and balanced daily stock to maximize
profits. Generated a 50% sales increase above preceding year.

Sales Training
Developed a Video Training program used in Branch Stores for new department
managers and sales people. Formal programs were extremely effective tools,
affording the participant a thorough understanding of the products supported with
current information and sales techniques.

1982 - 1986   UNIVERSITY OF CINCINNATI   Cincinnati, OH

Promotion and Public Relations
Produced distinguished university lecture series. Personally negotiated and
directed a campaign to have a figure of high national interest speak at the
university. Worked closely with Cincinnati Public Information Center. Coordinated
national and local press conference, handled all contract negotiations, arranged
promotion, all public relations with community and press, box office arrangements,
and hospitality for speakers. Supervised staff of 25.

1982 - 1984   COLLEGE MARKETING RESEARCH CORPORATION   Cincinnati, OH

Market Research
Conducted studies for the College Marketing Research Corporation, a division of
Playboy Enterprises. Distributed 30 major publications to paperback publishers,
resulting in improved circulation of books and magazines. Supervised staff of 15.

SALES/RETAIL

Cynthia's job title was not impressive, but her accomplishments were, so she used the functional format.

CYNTHIA CONNELLY
35 Waverly Court
San Francisco, CA 94507
(415) 682-3177

SALES/RETAIL:
- Managed over 100 East Coast accounts for large West Coast gourmet club.
- Developed promotional campaigns for new product lines.
- Increased sales by $500,000 in nine-month period.
- Coordinated accounts of over 20 large department stores.
- Sold specialty clothing for West Coast shop dealing with special, hard-to-fit clients.

MANAGEMENT:
- Organized and implemented a program for 40 college students abroad.
- Coordinated student/faculty liaison relationship.
- Managed an inventory of several thousand items.
- Trained and supervised three assistants.

WRITING:
- Wrote several free-lance articles published in a California daily.
- Composed correspondence in French as well as English.
- Fluent reading, writing, and speaking French, Spanish, and Italian.

EXPERIENCE:

| 1986 - Present | COQ AU VIN GOURMET CLUB
Promotional Sales | Tiburon, CA |
| 1986 | LA PANACHE BOUTIQUE
Salesperson | San Francisco, CA |

EDUCATION:

| 1986 | UNIVERSITY OF CALIFORNIA AT BERKELEY
B.A. degree - Liberal Arts | |

SECRETARY

Sandra stayed with chronological, as she was keeping the same target.

SANDRA GRUEN
South Broad Street
New Orleans, LA 70183
(504) 456-9923

EXCEPTION:

EXPERIENCE:

1986 - Present   GENERAL PACKAGING COMPANY
New Orleans, LA

Technical Secretary

Handled word processing for department of nine.
Composed correspondence and issued shipping
forms. Organized and maintained over 350
technical files with accounting cross-references.
Recorded incoming shipments and prepared
outgoing shipping forms for samples.

1984 - 1986   GERBEL ENGINEERING CORPORATION
New Orleans, LA

Bookkeeper

Processed accounts payable checks for real estate
properties. Paid real estate taxes, insurance
premiums, and utilities for real estate. Prepared
financial statements. Organized and submitted
monthly reports. Prepaid insurance premiums.
Typed yearly financial statements for corporation.

1982   SALVATION ARMY
New Orleans, LA

Office Manager

Supervised office functions, including supplies
purchasing, and clerical functions. Raised
$260,000 for new community center. Set up
computer systems. Designed forms, prepared
news releases, letters, and acknowledgements.
Recorded donations and pledges made by
corporations, organizations, and individuals.

EDUCATION:

1984   PROFESSIONAL SCHOOL FOR BUSINESS
New Orleans, LA   Major: Real Estate

SECURITIES ANALYST

JOSHUA A. MARGOLIS
72 Beuer Court
Cambridge, MA 02140
(617) 247-8299

EXPERIENCE:

1977 - Present   ARNOLD BURNHAM & COMPANY   Boston, MA

Senior Analyst

- Conducted statistical analyses of information affecting investment program of public, industrial, and financial institutions.
- Interpreted data concerning investment prices, yields, stability, and future trends using daily stock and bond reports, financial periodicals, and securities manuals.
- Researched and analyzed losses and adverse financial trends.
- Devised "value line" for utility stocks based on relationship of dividends to bond interest rates.
- Acted as chief analyst in textile industry.

1965 - 1977   GEMSTONE SILK, INC.   New York, NY

Chief Executive

- Complete responsibility for firm-wide sales of $10 million, including textile weaving, converting, and marketing.
- Developed processing innovations resulting in substantial cost reductions.
- As Vice President, set up data processing system for inventory and production control and sales analysis.
- Also held positions of Vice President, Plant Manager, and Technician.
- As Plant Manager, initiated new testing program for laboratory standards.
- As Technician, developed new materials for use in Navy aircraft.

EDUCATION:

1980   M.I.T. - Investment Analysis

1979   NEW YORK INSTITUTE OF FINANCE - Portfolio Management

1975   NEW YORK UNIVERSITY - Linear Programming

SOCIAL WORKER

Uses chronological, as he is staying in the same career area.

SAMUEL H. GREEN
387 PELHAM ROAD
NEW ROCHELLE, NY 10805
(914) 633-7875

1981 - Present

WESTCHESTER COUNTY PAROLE BOARD
Pelham, NY

<u>Narcotics Parole Officer</u>

Engaged in the rehabilitation of an average caseload of 40 certified addicts. Developed individualized programs for each client, according to need. This involved one-on-one counseling as well as frequent contact with client's family, incorporating them into treatment plan.

Created jobs for clients through contact with community agencies such as Operation Upgrade and Cellblock Theatre. Provided training in basic job skills, as well as additional education through local community programs such as Operation Comeback and Office of Vocational Rehabilitation.

1974 - 1981

WESTCHESTER COUNTY - DEPT. OF SOCIAL SERVICES
Hawthorne, NY

<u>Casework Supervisor/Caseworker</u>

Supervised five caseworkers in two years. Instructed them in agency procedures and casework techniques. Responsible for managing 300 active cases in the unit. Maintained controls for numerous required reports. Created time management system for employees to organize their work for maximum productivity.

Provided needed services as a caseworker for families seeking public assistance. Counseled clients individually, gearing the goal to fit each need. Set up special services such as homemakers for the aged and blind. Implemented plans such as employment, basic education, and nursing homes. Maintained accurate and complete records on each client.

Achieved highest record in casework unit in one year for clients' removal from public assistance roles.

<u>EDUCATION</u>:

1974

ST. JOHN'S UNIVERSITY - Long Island, NY
B.B.A.

TEACHER

JAN LEAH ERMAN
1540 42nd Street
Brooklyn, NY 11218
(718) 564-1217 - msg.

JOB TARGET: READING CONSULTANT - ELEMENTARY SCHOOLS

CAPABILITIES:

* Prepare outlines for daily and monthly course of study.
* Lecture and demonstrate with audiovisual teaching aids.
* Prepare, administer, and correct reading tests.
* Maintain order and discipline in large and small classes.
* Counsel and direct children with reading difficulties.
* Counsel parents and direct them into remedial action for specific cognitive or emotional problems of children.
* Train and develop children in verbal self-expression.

ACHIEVEMENTS:

* Trained two learning-disabled children to achieve full integration in public school class within two weeks.
* Tutored six "underachievers" in remedial reading; all six finished in upper 20% of class by end of year.
* Developed new system for reporting reading comprehension analyses now used in school system city-wide.
* Introduced audiovisual techniques for math learning into Grade 2 with great success.
* Cited as Teacher of The Year in 1986 in a school of 800 students.

WORK HISTORY:

1982 - Present   YESHIVA HAVRAM SECULAR DIVISION
                  Brooklyn, NY

                  Fifth & Sixth Grade Teacher

1981   DOWD COMMUNICATIONS
                  New York, NY

                  Production Assistant

EDUCATION: NEW YORK UNIVERSITY
                  1985 - M.S. in Education; Emphasis on Reading in Elementary Schools
                  1981 - B.A. in Sociology; Minor in Elementary Education

---

TRAVEL AGENT

ELLEN T. LONDOFF

450 Fort Washington Avenue
New York, NY 10033
(212) 668-3470

WORK EXPERIENCE

1985 - Present   LEISURE TRAVEL SALES, INC.   New York, NY

<u>Sales/Marketing</u>: Develop wholesale travel department. Focus on individual and group travel programs for executives, employees, groups, civic, and fraternal organizations. Design incentive programs for sales force within several companies.

<u>Advertising</u>: Evaluate profitability of advertising strategy. Responsible for selecting best vehicles for copy and promotion. Utilize demographical information and readership data of trade publications and journals for determining advertising campaign. Personally write advertising copy for major ads.

<u>Research</u>: Examine which specific facilities and destinations would best service each group's style, budget, and conference needs. Survey industries, and developed individual presentations for conference planning.

<u>Budgeting</u>: Plan budgets for each program. Negotiate hotel contracts. Cost out internal operational expenses (reservations, documentation, ticketing, itinerary planning). Budget out advertising expenditures from copywriting to final printing and placement stages. Reduced operational costs by 20% in first year of program.

1981 - 1985   BIGGER MAN APPAREL, INC.   Orange, CT

<u>Customer Service Representative</u>

Responsible for all manufacturing sources meeting delivery deadline obligations. Functions included merchandising, pricing, buying, and general sales. Worked on all phases of company advertising.

EDUCATION

1981   ADELPHI UNIVERSITY   Garden City, NY
B.A., Liberal Arts

INTERNATIONAL INVESTMENT BANKER

CAROLE PALKA
56 MARKHAM PLACE
LONDON W3
(044-1) 234-0992

WORK EXPERIENCE:

1986 - Present   CHASE INVESTMENT BANK, LONDON, U.K.
                   Managing Director
                   •Arranged a $500 million multiple option facility for the
                    Kingdom of Spain.
                   •Originated ten Eurobond issues throughout the EEC for U.S.
                    and European multinationals.
                   •Arranged and syndicated a ten-year S.F. $100 million loan
                    swap transaction.

1978 - 1986   THE CHASE MANHATTAN BANK N.A., NEW YORK, NY

1983 - 1986   Vice President - Swiss Institutional Banking
                   •Managed eleven person team overseeing employer's
                    relationship with 150 Swiss and Liechtenstein banks.
                   •Negotiated over $100 million in new documentary business.
                   •Coordinated five-year European Strategic Plan.

1981 - 1983   Vice President - International Trade Finance
                   •Created and implemented innovative approach to extending
                    credit in conjunction with the World Bank.
                   •Developed new financial risk participation product to increase
                    trade finance business.
                   •Coordinated employer's worldwide financial activities with
                    World Bank and IMF.

1978 - 1981   Second Vice President - Corporate Foreign Direct Investment
                   •Managed employer's relationship with U.S. subsidiaries of French
                    and Swiss multinationals.
                   •Developed $30 million portfolio of high quality financial assets.
                   •Directed marketing that resulted in 20% increase in fee business.

EDUCATION:
1978   M.B.A., NEW YORK UNIVERSITY, New York, NY
1974   B.A., WILLIAMS COLLEGE, Williamstown, MA

LANGUAGE
SKILL: Fluent in French - read, speak, write.

RESEARCH ASSISTANT

LUDWIG JOHANNESEN
Purdue University
Windsor Halls, Box 356
West Lafayette, IN 47907
(317) 495-6945

EDUCATION:

1985 - 1989 PURDUE UNIVERSITY
B.A. - May, 1989
Major: Psychology. GPA = 3.45
Pertinent Courses: Advanced Statistical Analysis, Experimental
Psychology.

Spring 1988 STANFORD UNIVERSITY - Business School
Semester study with pertinent courses in Industrial/Organizational
Psychology, Human Resources Management, Human Factors in
Engineering; independent research on mentor-protégé relationships in the
work environment; independent research on levels of moral development in
group decision making.

EMPLOYMENT:

1986 - Present COLGATE UNIVERSITY   Hamilton, NY

Research Assistant - Psychology Department

- Coordinate experiments for professional research data collection.
- Schedule experiments, as well as running subjects through
  paradigms.
- Analyze data of preliminary findings via computer.
- Train other assistants on procedures for running experiments.

1986 ALLIED-SIGNAL CORPORATION   Morristown, NJ

Summer Intern - Corporate Human Resources Department

- Analyzed data concerning problems with the performance
  evaluation system and generated solutions in light of corporate
  policy.
- Developed feedback information on the performance evaluation
  system for employees.
- Experienced the various aspects of human resources management
  (i.e., personnel, compensation, employee evaluation).
- Acquired knowledge of corporate college relations and recruiting
  procedures.

ACTIVITIES:

Since 1985
- Purdue University Peer Counseling and Referral Service -
  counselor and budget coordinator, as well as original founder.
- Anchorperson for Purdue University's television station.

EXECUTIVE ASSISTANT—INTERNATIONAL

MIRIAM CARROSA
3065 Central Avenue, Apt. 14-M
Fort Lee, NJ 07024
(201) 583-1418

1981 - 1988	UARCO PETROLEUM CORPORATION	New York, NY

Assistant to Vice President - Foreign Personnel

- Performed annual studies on cost-saving projects which minimized expenditures incurred in employee relocation. These included housing facilities, automobile rentals/purchases, and traveling. Made recommendations to upper level management to maximize efficiency of company's relocation policies.
- Obtained and analyzed quotes from different moving companies specializing in shipments to foreign locations. Awarded contract resulting in 10% cost reduction.
- In conjunction with legal department, researched and prepared an updated "Policy and Procedure Manual," which supplied necessary information about company and foreign country of residence. Processed manual through WANG word processing.
- Served as liaison between company and foreign consulates for the acquisition of visas and other accreditation.
- Prepared monthly payroll of $370,000 for 85 internationally based employees. Compiled all supporting documentation and calculated foreign and domestic tax data. Submitted tax information to IRS on a quarterly and/or yearly basis (i.e., 940, 941, W-2, and 1099).

1979 - 1981	DU PONT CHEMICALS, INC.	New York, NY

Executive Assistant - Director of Operations

- Calculated capital requests from departments/divisions that provided management with initial financial information for new projects and maintenance of fixed assets.
- Researched and prioritized demands to comply with government regulations in conjunction with OSHA representative.

1976 - 1979	WALTER KIDDE & COMPANY	New York, NY

Accounting Clerk - General Accounting Department
Secretary to Assistant Controller

- Performed miscellaneous secretarial functions: statistical typing, filing, telephone screening, and setting up meetings. In addition, served as Accounts Payable Clerk.

EDUCATION: Candidate for B.A. in Business Administration with concentration in Accounting & Finance at New York University (May, 1989)
GPA = 3.80; Dean's List all semesters.

AFFILIATIONS/
MEMBERSHIPS: Board of Directors of Co-op; active member of Big Sisters; tutor students in Accounting and Spanish at NYU.

SPECIAL SKILLS: Bilingual English/Spanish - written and verbal translation experience.

PROGRAM MANAGER

MARIBETH SIMON

195 Overlook Avenue   (914) 739-8868 - message
Peekskill, NY 10566   (914) 769-3017 - work

WORK EXPERIENCE

CRESTLINE COMMUNICATIONS - Pleasantville, NY   1987 - Present

Program Manager

Manage a customer service/marketing program targeting the company's top customers
nationally, resulting in $437,008 sales per year. Identify opportunities, formulate
strategies, and implement plans to stimulate sales of company's microcomputer software
product line. Supervise staff of four.

GROUP HEALTH ASSOCIATES - Seattle, WA   1980 - 1986

Administrative Analyst II   1986

Developed decision papers for trustees and executives of $360 million budget HMO.
Identified organizational impact of issues and recommended alternative options. Edited
managerial materials for presentation to board, consulting with senior level executives in
the development of information.

Assistant Office Director   1980 - 1985

Supervised staff of six. Oversaw transition of office to fully automated office system,
resulting in increased staff productivity and higher morale. Wrote newsletters and speeches
for trustees. Developed and refined a computerized data base management program,
improving the speed in retrieving information used in decision-making. Managed a
reduction in staff due to organizational budget cuts, maintaining productivity standard with
fewer staff members.

AMERICAN ASSN OF RETIRED PERSONS - Washington, DC   1979 - 1980

Legislative Specialist

Researched, analyzed, and reported legislative interests of association's membership.
Organized association's first formal legislative correspondence section, improving response
time to over 500 letters received each month.

EDUCATION

1986   UNIVERSITY OF WASHINGTON - Seattle, WA
              Master of Public Administration

1975   ELMIRA COLLEGE - Elmira, NY
              B.A., Political Science, cum laude

MANUFACTURING PLANNER
SHOWS COMPANY BUYOUT

Douglas Fredricks
82 Linden Street
Allentown, PA 18103
(215) 435-7934

WORK EXPERIENCE:

1984 - Present	BLACK & DECKER — Allentown, Pennsylvania
1952 - 1984	GENERAL ELECTRIC COMPANY — Allentown, Pennsylvania, Housewares Manufacturing Department

1977 - Present

Senior Manufacturing Planner
- Established work methods and work measurements. Procured equipment to manufacture Allentown products safely at low cost.
- Collaborated on setting realistic and challenging operation goals.
- Cited by senior management for achieving highest productivity goals in sixth year on the job.
- Planned and established approved revisions in operations, equipment, and tools to accommodate production schedule changes, product mix, or design changes.
- Analyzed methods, facilities, and processes leading to lower manufacturing costs.
- Coordinated task forces for cost reduction.

1969 - 1977

Manufacturing Engineer
- Evaluated and appraised changes to and deviations from design, materials, and specifications.
- Investigated customer complaints and recommended corrective action.
- Evaluated product designs and applications.
- Analyzed prototype models of housewares products. Determined manufacturing specifications, and cost projections.

1960 - 1969

Methods Engineer
- Specified manufacturing processes.
- Utilized predetermined standard data, methods analysis, and work samplings for providing shop operations with instructions and time standards.

1952 - 1960

Lab Technician
- Handled simple, technical, analytical procedures.

EDUCATION: HIGH SCHOOL GRADUATE

HUMAN RESOURCES
RECENT GRADUATE

SANDRA MANNICKS
174-B Van Cortlandt Park South
Bronx, NY 10463
(212) 726-2994

EDUCATION:

1986 - 1988   COLUMBIA BUSINESS SCHOOL   New York, NY
M.B.A., Organizational Effectiveness - May, 1988
Beta Sigma Phi; Dean's List. Named MacMannus Scholar for 1986-87 school year.
President, Human Resources Management Club.

1980 - 1984   SWARTHMORE COLLEGE   Swarthmore, PA
B.A., Biology - May, 1984
Vice President, Class of 1984. Resident Assistant for hall of 44 students. Served on two
student council committees. Varsity field hockey, basketball, and lacrosse. Photography
editor, college yearbook.

Spring 1982   MARINER EDUCATION ASSOCIATION   Woods Hole, MA
Completed marine biology and oceanography program. Spent six weeks ashore and six
weeks at sea. Elected class representative.

EXPERIENCE:

Summer 1987 CITICORP   New York, NY
Corporate Human Resources Summer Intern

Created a clearinghouse of training programs offered throughout Citicorp worldwide.
Helped organize and conduct an all-day orientation program for newly hired human
resources professionals. Designed a recruiting brochure. Devised a system for evaluating
the mentor program for new hires.

1984 - 1986   BRONX HIGH SCHOOL OF SCIENCE   Bronx, NY
High School Teacher

Taught Biology, Earth Science, Psychology. Advised 27 students. Set up
photomicrography laboratory. Implemented senior psychology seminars. Coached
lacrosse.

Summer 1985 MARINE BIOLOGY LABORATORIES   Woods Hole, MA
Research Technician

Performed laboratory and library research on marine invertebrates. Co-authored several
papers.
Summers
1979 - 1984   SEASIDE LOBSTER HUT   Wellfleet, MA
Manager

Trained, directed, and supervised 43 employees in a busy resort area restaurant.
Responsible for public relations, general organization, purchasing supplies, and monitoring
food quality.

ADDITIONAL INFORMATION: Listed in *Who's Who in Professional and Executive Women*,
1988 Edition. Member, ALMACA. Hold Secondary School Teacher's Certification in Biology. Have
lived in China and Turkey.

TELEMARKETER

Lynne Chase
15 Bluff Road
Fort Lee, NJ 07043
(201) 850-2312

WORK EXPERIENCE:

Management	• Supervised 20-person telephone sales program.
	• Developed strategic marketing plan.
	• Trained telephone sales personnel.
	• Recruited and hired sales and clerical personnel.

Marketing & Sales
- Increased sales of college textbooks by 15% in assigned territory.
- Conducted cold-calling campaign and developed new market for professional newsletter.
- Named "Telemarketer of the month" for four consecutive months.

Organization & Planning
- Developed monthly sales plans, setting group and individual targets.
- Determined budget and tracked profitably.
- Organized and implemented special promotional telephone campaign.

WORK HISTORY:

1984 — Present	SIMON & SCHUSTER, Englewood Cliffs, N.J.
1987 — Present	Telemarketing Manager, Textbook Division
1984 — 1987	Telemarketing Representative

EDUCATION:

| 1984 | Pennsylvania State University, B.A. |

CONSULTANT/ENTREPRENEUR

209 East 56th Street
New York, N.Y. 10022
April 12, 1989

Mrs. Marian Flynn
Vice President
Sogin Corporation
883 Third Avenue
New York, N.Y. 10022

Dear Mrs. Flynn:

Dan Jensen at Citibank suggested I contact you concerning the announcement of Sogin's redundancy program scheduled for later this year.

When a large organization such as yours is faced with downsizing, it is often helpful to have an outside or neutral party involved in the outplacement of employees. My extensive experience in working with situations similar to yours could be beneficial to you. I handled a large portion of the outplacement work for AT&T at the time of divestiture, and I am sensitive to the feelings and needs of both sides. I would like to meet with you to discuss ways in which I could support you in your efforts to assist your employees through this difficult transition.

I will telephone your office next Tuesday to arrange a convenient time to get together.

Sincerely,

Eileen Martin

Eileen Martin

CONSULTANT/ENTREPRENEUR

EILEEN MARTIN

209 East 56th Street
New York, NY 10022
(212) 895-0990

SUMMARY OF ACCOMPLISHMENTS

- Co-produced managers' leadership development program for General Dynamics in October, 1987.

- Former partner/owner of Career Dynamics, Inc.

- Partner for twelve years to noted career development expert.

- Published in *Working Woman* magazine in 1985 and 1982 four articles on resume-writing and how to survive being fired.

- Led over 200 workshops in outplacement and early retirement for employees ranging in levels from blue collar to senior executives.

- Successfully counseled over 150 individual job-seekers in private custom-designed sessions. Emphasis on women and entrepreneurs.

- Lecturer at over forty college campuses on job-finding techniques and philosophy.

- Edited and test-marketed over sixteen career-related programs in ten years with Career Dynamics, Inc.

- Trained numerous workshop leaders in the U.S.A. and Europe to deliver various career-related programs.

- Client company list (partial):

      General Dynamics
      Goodyear Tire & Rubber
      Colgate-Palmolive
      Kodak
      Polaroid
      New York Life Insurance Company
      AT&T
      New York Telephone

SAMPLE RESUME PARAGRAPHS

On the following pages we have included sample paragraphs relating to occupational titles not fully covered in the sample resumes themselves. Use them as needed in creating your own resume.

ACCOUNT EXECUTIVE

Plan, coordinate, and direct advertising campaign for clients of advertising agency. Consult with client to determine advertising requirements and budgetary limitations, utilizing knowledge of product or service to be advertised, media capabilities, and audience characteristics.

Consult with creative staff, photographers, and other media production specialists to select media to be used and to estimate costs. Submit proposal, including estimated budget to client for approval.

Coordinate marketing research, copywriting, layout, media-buying, display, and promotional activities to successfully implement campaign.

ACTIVITIES PLANNER—COLLEGE

Provide motivation and successful sales targeting for a team of assistant box office managers. Manage ticket sales by coordinating mini-box offices to open in time segments so that tickets are available sixteen hours per day. Schedule sports events during college years. Produce large sellout for dances and other social events.

ADMINISTRATIVE ASSISTANT

Provide support to management by handling all routine and administrative work such as coordinating office services, preparing budgets and cash flow statements, maintaining records, tracing information, coordinating details of business trips, and organizing special projects. Communicate with counterparts in other departments and retrieve information through establishing a network. Conduct research, provide facts and statistics for reports. Read and condense lengthy documents.

ART DIRECTOR

Formulate concepts and supervise staff in executing layout designs for artwork and copy to be presented by visual communications media, such as magazines, books, newspapers, television, posters, and packaging. Review illustrative material and consult with client or individual responsible for presentation regarding budget, background information, objectives, presentation approaches, style, techniques, and related production factors.

Formulate layout and design concept, select and secure suitable illustrative material, or conceive and delegate production of material and detail to artists and photographers. Assign and direct staff members to develop design concepts into art layouts and prepare layouts for printing. Review, approve, and present final layouts to client or department head for approval.

BIOTECHNOLOGIST

Conduct research and development activities to augment knowledge of living organisms. Employ genetic knowledge and technology to recombine the genetic material of plants and animals. Perform studies and assay development for new drug discovery projects. Conduct computer assisted analyses of data. Monitor and report on progress of ongoing clinical studies.

CERTIFIED PUBLIC ACCOUNTANT

Examine clients' financial records and reports and attest to their conformity with standards of preparation and reporting. Prepare income tax returns and advise clients of the tax advantages and disadvantages of certain business decisions. Consult on a variety of matters, such as revising the clients' accounting systems to better meet their needs and advising clients on managing cash resources more profitably. Prepare financial reports to meet public disclosure requirements of stock exchanges, the SEC, and other regulatory bodies.

COMPUTER ANIMATOR

Create sophisticated computer graphics using supercomputers such as the Cray X-MP digital image producer. "Paint" on computer VDT via a digitalizing tablet to enhance and speed the development of animation and other presentations. Draw electronically using a mouse cursor control. Store and retrieve two-dimensional images, text and lettering to be captured on slides, film, video, or hard copy.

CORPORATE FOUNDATION MANAGER

Administer the distribution of funding to nonprofit organizations. Meet with organizations seeking grants, administer requests, prepare agenda for corporate meeting, and follow up on gifts. Coordinate employee participations. Act as liaison with the community. Maintain accounting records using computer spreadsheet software package.

COUNSELING DIRECTOR

Direct personnel engaged in providing educational and vocational guidance for students and graduates. Assign and evaluate work of personnel. Conduct in-service training program for professional staff. Coordinate counseling bureau with school and community services. Analyze counseling and guidance procedures and techniques to improve quality of service.

Counsel individuals and groups relative to personal and social problems, and educational and vocational objectives. Address community groups and faculty members to interpret counseling service. Supervise maintenance of occupational library for use by counseling personnel. Direct activities of testing and occupational service center.

DENTAL HYGIENIST

Provide preventive dental care and encourage patients to develop good oral hygiene skills. Evaluate patients' dental health. Remove calculus, stain, and placque and apply caries-preventive agents such as fluoride and pit and fissure sealants. Instruct patients on placque control. Expose and develop dental x rays. Place temporary fillings and periodontal dressings. Remove sutures. Polish and recontour amalgam restorations. Administer local anesthetics.

DRAFTER

Prepare clear, complete, and accurate working plans and detailed drawings from rough or detailed sketches or notes for engineering or manufacturing purposes, according to specified dimensions. Make final drawing and specifications, checking dimension of parts, materials to be used, relation of one part to another, and relations of various parts to whole structure or project. Exercise manual skill in manipulation of triangle, T-square, and other drafting tools or make drawings on videoscreens using new CAD/CAM system. Draw charts for representation of statistical data. Draw finished designs from sketches. Utilize knowledge of various machines, engineering practices, mathematics, building materials, and other physical sciences to complete drawings.

ECONOMIST

Utilize knowledge of economic relationships to advise businesses, government agencies, and others. Devise methods and procedures to obtain needed data, including sampling techniques, to conduct surveys. Employ econometric modeling to develop projections. Review and analyze relevant data;

prepare tables and charts; prepare clear, concise reports. Analyze the effect of tax law changes. Prepare economic and business forecasts. Provide information to support management decision-making process.

EDITORIAL ASSISTANT

Prepare written material for publication. Review copy to detect errors in spelling, punctuation, and syntax. Verify facts, dates, and statistics, using standard reference sources. Assure that manuscripts conform to publisher's style and editorial policy and mark copy for typesetter, using standard symbols to indicate how type should be set.

Read galley and pageproofs to detect errors and indicate corrections, using standard proofreading symbols. Confer with authors regarding changes made to manuscript. Select and crop photographs and illustrative materials to conform to space and subject matter requirements.

EDUCATIONAL THERAPIST

Teach elementary and secondary school subjects to educationally handicapped students with neurological or emotional disabilities in schools, institutions, or other specialized facilities. Plan curriculum and prepare lessons and other instructional materials to meet individual needs of students, considering factors such as physical, emotional, and educational levels of development. Instruct students in specific subject areas, such as English, mathematics, and geography.

Observe students for signs of disruptive behavior, such as violence, outbursts of temper, and episodes of destructiveness. Counsel students with regard to disruptive behavior, utilizing a variety of therapeutic methods. Confer with other staff members to plan programs designed to promote educational, physical, and social development of students.

ENVIRONMENTAL HEALTH INSPECTOR

Ensure that food, water, and air meet government standards. Check the cleanliness and safety of food and beverages produced in dairies and processing plants, served in restaurants, hospitals, and other institutions. Examine the handling, processing, and serving of food for compliance with sanitation rules and regulations.

Oversee the treatment and disposal of sewage and refuse. Examine places where there is danger of pollution. Collect samples of air and water for analysis. Determine the nature and cause of pollution and initiate action to stop it.

FASHION COORDINATOR

Promote new fashions and coordinate promotional activities, such as fashion shows, to induce consumer acceptance. Study fashion and trade journals, travel to garment centers, attend fashion shows, and visit manufacturers and merchandise markets to obtain information on fashion trends. Consult with buying personnel to gain advice regarding types of fashions store will purchase and feature for season. Advise publicity and display departments of merchandise to be publicized.

Select garments and accessories to be shown at fashion shows. Provide information on current fashions, style trends, and use of accessories. Contract with models, musicians, caterers, and other personnel to manage staging of shows.

GUIDANCE DIRECTOR

Organize, administer, and coordinate guidance program in public school system. Formulate guidance policies and procedures. Plan and conduct in-service training program for guidance workers and selected teachers. Plan and supervise testing program in school system and devise and direct use of records, reports, and other material essential to program.

Supervise school placement service. Establish and supervise maintenance of occupational libraries in schools. Coordinate guidance activities with community agencies and other areas of school system. Conduct or supervise research studies to evaluate effectiveness of guidance program.

GUIDANCE NAVIGATION CONTROL ENGINEER

Develop basic design concepts used in the design, development, and validation of electromechanical GNC systems for stabilizing, navigating, and maneuvering vehicles in flight. Provide analysis for satellites and space launch vehicles. Employ knowledge and experience in rigid body dynamics, guidance, digital flight controls, and flight control computer software validation.

INDUSTRIAL ELECTRONIC EQUIPMENT REPAIRER

Install and repair electronic equipment used in industrial automated equipment controls, missile control systems, medical and diagnostic equipment, transmitters and antennas. Set up and service an industrial robotics system. Use testing equipment to ensure everything is functioning properly before the customer takes charge of the equipment. Perform preventive maintenance; check, clean, and repair equipment periodically. Maintain a log on each piece of equipment indicating the date and its condition, and when it is to be serviced again. Determine the cause of equipment breakdown using tools such as voltameter, ohmmeter, signal generator, ammeter, and oscilloscope. Repair and replace defective components and wiring, and calibrate the equipment.

INTERNAL AUDITOR

Examine and evaluate the firm's financial and information systems, management procedures, and internal controls. Ensure that records are accurate and controls adequate to protect against fraud and waste. Review the company's operations and evaluate their efficiency, effectiveness, and compliance with corporate policies, laws, and government regulations. Monitor controls in computer software to ensure reliability of systems and integrity of data. Correct problems with software systems and develop special programs to meet unique needs.

LOBBYIST

Contact and confer with members of legislature and other holders of public office to persuade them to support legislation favorable to clients' interests. Study proposed legislation to determine possible effect on interest of clients, who may be a person, specific group, or general public. Confer with legislators and officials to emphasize supposed weaknesses or merits of specific bills to influence passage, defeat, or amendment of measure or introduction of legislation more favorable to clients' interests.

Contact individuals and groups having similar interests in order to encourage them also to contact legislators and present views. Prepare news releases and informational pamphlets and conduct news conferences in order to state clients' views and to inform public of features of proposed legislation considered desirable or undesirable.

MANAGEMENT CONSULTANT

Help solve a vast array of organizational problems. Consult with client to define the nature and extent of the project. Collect and review data. Analyze statistics and other data, interview employees, observe the operations on a day-to-day basis. Utilize knowledge of theory, principles, or technology of specific discipline or field of specialization to determine solutions. Prepare recommendations and write a report of findings. Make formal oral presentations to the client. Assist in the implementation of proposals.

MANAGEMENT TRAINEE

Perform assigned duties, under close direction of experienced personnel, to gain knowledge and experience required for promotion to management positions. Receive training and perform duties in departments, such as credit, customer relations, accounting, or sales to become familiar with line and staff functions that affect each phase of business.

Observe and study techniques and traits of experienced workers in order to acquire knowledge of methods, procedures, and standards required for performance of departmental duties.

MANAGER, RETAIL STORE

Manage retail store engaged in selling specific line of merchandise, as groceries, meat, liquor, apparel, jewelry, or furniture; related lines of merchandise, as radios, televisions, and household appliances; or general line of merchandise.

Perform following duties personally or supervise staff performing duties. Plan and prepare work schedules and assign employees to specific duties. Formulate pricing policies on merchandise according to requirements for profitability of store operations. Coordinate sales promotion activities and prepare, or direct workers preparing, merchandise displays and advertising copy.

Supervise employees engaged in, or performing, sales work, taking of inventories, reconciling cash with sales receipts, keeping operating records, or preparing daily record of transactions for accountant. Order merchandise or prepare requisitions to replenish merchandise on hand. Ensure compliance of employees with established security, sales, and record-keeping procedures and practices.

MARKETING MANAGER

Analyze and evaluate marketing research data and apply to customer base. Plan and develop marketing strategies. Coordinate with product management on product design. Develop and manage cross-product marketing materials. Design promotional programs; supervise sales training. Develop and manage budgets. Work with ad agencies, type houses, editors, printers, art directors, producers, and audiovisual studios. Coordinate public relations materials and execute press releases for new products. Oversee scheduling and participation in trade shows and develop required promotional materials.

MECHANICAL ENGINEER

Design and develop power producing machines such as internal combustion engines, steam and gas turbines and jet and rocket engines, refrigeration and air conditioning equipment, robots, machine tools, materials handling systems, and industrial production equipment. Direct and coordinate operation and repair activities.

MEDICAL RECORD ADMINISTRATOR

Plan, develop, and administer medical record systems for hospital, clinic, health center, or similar facility, to meet standards of accrediting and regulatory agencies. Collect and analyze patient and institutional data. Assist medical staff in evaluating quality of patient care and in developing criteria and methods for such evaluation.

Develop and implement policies and procedures for documenting, storing, and retrieving information and for processing medical-legal documents, insurance, and correspondence requests, in conformance with federal, state, and local statutes. Develop in-service educational materials and conduct instructional programs for health care personnel. Supervise staff in preparing and analyzing medical documents. Provide consultant services to health care facilities, health data Systems, related health organizations, and governmental agencies. Engage in basic and applied research in health care field. Testify in court about records and record procedures. Train and supervise medical records staff.

MERCHANDISE MANAGER

Formulate merchandising policies and coordinate merchandising activities in wholesale or retail establishment. Determine markup and markdown percentages necessary to ensure profit based on estimated budget, profit goals, and average rate of stock turnover. Determine amount of merchandise to be stocked and direct buyers in purchase of supplies for resale. Consult with other personnel to plan sales promotion programs.

NUCLEAR MEDICINE TECHNOLOGIST

Perform activities involving the use of radionuclides in the diagnosis and treatment of disease. Develop and administer procedures for the purchase, use, and disposal of radioactive nuclides. Calculate, prepare, and administer the correct dosage of radiopharmaceuticals for the patient to take. Operate the gamma scintillation scanner and other diagnostic imaging equipment and view the images on computer, screen, or film. Process cardiac function studies with the aid of a computer. Perform ultrasound scans, fluoroscopy, and x rays. Collect body specimens such as blood and urine and measure for radioactivity. Ensure that safety procedures required by the Nuclear Regulatory Commission are carefully followed. Do research and conduct laboratory studies. Maintain complete and accurate records.

NUMERICAL CONTROL TOOL PROGRAMMER

Apply a broad knowledge of machinery operations, mathematics, and the working properties of metal and plastics used to make parts. Analyze blueprints. Plan and design the sequence of machine operations and select proper cutting tools. Write the program in the language of the machine's controller using a CAD/CAM system.

PACKAGE DESIGNER

Design containers for products, such as foods, beverages, toiletries, cigarettes, and medicines. Confer with representatives of engineering, marketing, management, and other departments to determine packaging requirements and type of product market. Sketch design of container for specific product, considering factors such as attractiveness, convenience in handling and storing, distinctiveness for identification by consumer, and simplicity to minimize production costs.

Render design, including exterior markings and labels, using paints and brushes. Typically fabricate model in paper, wood, glass, plastic, or metal, depending on material to be used in package. Make modifications required by approving authority.

PLANT ENGINEER

Direct and coordinate, through engineering and supervisory personnel, activities concerned with design, construction, and maintenance of equipment in accordance with engineering principles and safety regulations. Directly oversee maintenance of plant buildings. Coordinate re-surveys, new designs, and maintenance schedules with operating requirements. Prepare bid sheets and contracts for construction and facilities acquisition. Test newly installed machines and equipment to ensure fulfillment of contract specifications.

PROJECT DIRECTOR

Plan, direct, and coordinate activities of designated project to ensure that aims, goals, or objectives specified for project are accomplished in accordance with prescribed priorities, time limitation, and funding conditions. Review project proposal or plan and determine methods and procedures for its accomplishment. Develop staffing plan and establish work plan and schedules for each phase of project in accordance with time limitations and funding.

Recruit or request assignment of personnel. Confer with staff, designate responsibilities, and establish scope of authority. Direct and coordinate activities of project through delegated subordinates and establish budget control system. Review project reports on status of each phase and modify schedules as required. Prepare project status reports for management. Confer with project personnel to provide technical advice and to assist in solving problems.

PUBLIC RELATIONS REPRESENTATIVE

Plan and conduct public relations program designed to create and maintain favorable public image for employer or client. Plan and direct development and communication of information designed to keep public informed of employer's programs, accomplishments, or point of view. Arrange for public relations efforts in order to meet needs, objectives, and policies of individual, special interest group, business concern, nonprofit organization, or governmental agency, serving as in-house staff member or as outside consultant.

Prepare and distribute fact sheets, news releases, photographs, scripts, motion pictures, or tape recordings to media representatives and other persons who may be interested in learning about or publicizing employer's activities or message. Purchase advertising space and time as required. Arrange for and conduct public-contact programs designed to meet employer's objectives; utilize knowledge of changing attitudes and opinions of consumers, client's employees, or other interest groups.

Promote goodwill through such publicity efforts as speeches, exhibits, films, tours, and question/answer sessions. Represent employer during community projects and at public, social, and business gatherings.

RESEARCH NUTRITIONIST

Conduct nutritional research to expand knowledge in one or more phases of dietetics. Plan, organize, and conduct programs in nutrition, foods, and food-service systems, evaluating and utilizing appropriate methodology and tools to carry out program. Study and analyze recent scientific discoveries in nutrition for application in current research, for development of tools for future research, and for interpretation to the public. Communicate findings through reports and publications.

RESIDENCE COUNSELOR

Provide individual and group guidance services relative to problems of scholastic, educational, and personal-social nature to dormitory students. Suggest remedial or corrective actions and assist students in making better adjustments and in intelligent planning of life goals. Plan and direct program to orient new students and assist in their integration into campus life. Initiate and conduct group conferences to plan and discuss programs and policies related to assignment of quarter, social and recreational activities, and dormitory living. Supervise dormitory activities. Investigate reports of misconduct and attempt to resolve or eliminate causes of conflict.

ROBOT TECHNICIAN

Assemble robotic prototypes. Work from engineer's CAD/CAM blueprints and create the first working model of the robot. Discover and troubleshoot system malfunctions. Evaluate retooling requirements for new products. Create cost analyses for adapting automation systems for new product design. Test and calibrate electronic test equipment.

SALES MANAGER

Direct the firm's sales program. Assign sales territories and goals. Establish training program for sales representatives. Oversee regional and local sales managers and staffs in larger firms. Maintain contact with dealers and distributors. Analyze sales statistics gathered by staff to monitor preferences and decide which products to continue or discontinue.

Order merchandise, supplies, and equipment as necessary. Ensure that merchandise is correctly priced and displayed. Prepare sales and inventory reports. Approve checks for payment of merchandise and issue credit or cash refund on returned merchandise. Plan department layout on merchandise or advertising display.

SOCIOLOGIST

Study human society and social behavior by examining groups and social institutions that people form. Study origin, growth, behavior, and interaction of groups. Collect information, assess validity, and analyze results. Conduct surveys or engage in direct observation to gather data. Utilize statistical and computer techniques in research. Evaluate social and welfare programs.

STUDENT AFFAIRS DIRECTOR

Plan and arrange social, cultural, and recreational activities of various student groups according to university policies and regulations. Meet with student and faculty groups to plan activities. Evaluate programs and suggest modifications. Schedule events to prevent overlapping and coordinate activities with sports and other university programs.

Contact caterers, entertainers, decorators, and others to arrange for scheduled events. Conduct orientation program for new students with other members of faculty and staff. Advise student groups on financial status of and methods for improving their organizations. Promote student participation in social, cultural, and recreational activities.

SYSTEMS ANALYST

Plan and develop methods for computerizing business and scientific tasks or improving the computer system already in use. Discuss data processing problems with managers or specialists to determine exact nature of the problem. Design goals of the system and use techniques such as mathematical model building, sampling, and cost accounting to plan the system.

Develop the design and prepare charts and diagrams that describe it in terms management can understand. Prepare cost benefit analysis and return on investment. Determine computer hardware and software needed. Prepare specifications for programmers. Design forms required to collect and distribute information.

Develop better procedures and adapt the system to handle additional types of data. Research and devise new methods for systems analysis.

TEACHER'S AIDE

Assist teaching staff of public or private elementary or secondary school by performing any combination of tasks in classroom. Help instruct children under the guidance and supervision of the teacher. Prepare lesson outline and plan where appropriate and submit it for review. Prepare and develop various teaching aids, such as bibliographies, charts, and graphs. Help and supervise students in classroom, cafeteria, and schoolyard. Record grades, set up equipment, help prepare materials for instruction. Grade tests and papers, check homework, and keep health and attendance records.

TELECOMMUNICATIONS SPECIALIST

Provide expert advice to companies on putting together the most efficient, effective and economical system. Be familiar with the telephone and data communications systems available from different manufacturers and the many ways to lease transmission lines. Have knowledge of computerized telephone systems, computerized mail, video conferencing, teletext, telex, and facsimile. Analyze the current system and the company's needs. Select and design a system to meet these needs. Supervise the installation. Establish a framework for its economical operation.

URBAN AND REGIONAL PLANNER

Develop programs to provide for the future growth or revitalization of urban, suburban, and rural communities and their regions. Examine community facilities to ensure they will meet the demands placed on them. Keep abreast of economic and legal issues and changes in housing and building codes and environmental regulations. Design new transportation systems and parking facilities. Project long-range needs for housing, transport, business, and industrial sites that may develop as a result of population growth and economic and social changes.

Analyze and propose alternative ways to achieve more efficient and attractive urban areas. Prepare detailed studies that show current use of land for residential, business, and community purposes. Provide information on the types of industries in the community, the characteristics of the population, the employment and economic trends. Propose ways to use undeveloped or underutilized land and design the layout of the recommended facilities and buildings. Demonstrate how the plan could be implemented and its costs.

WATER AND WASTEWATER TREATMENT PLANT OPERATOR

Control the processes and equipment used to remove solid materials, chemicals, and microorganisms from water or to render them harmless. Read and interpret meters and gauges and adjust controls. Operate chemical feeding devices. Take samples of water and perform chemical and biological laboratory analyses. Test and adjust the chlorine level in wastewater. Make minor repairs to valves, pumps, and other equipment. Use computers to help monitor equipment and processes. Read and interpret results.

Managing Your
Career Search

THE WORKLIFE REVOLUTION . . . AND YOU

You can make a difference in the quality of your worklife. It's as simple as that. As you expand your understanding of how the job market works, you will uncover a wide range of work possibilities and be more alert in how to interest these employers in your capabilities.

It is by understanding the rules of the job game, and igniting your own work consciousness, that you take a leading role in the worklife revolution and join the growing number of people who bring work and life into personal harmony—regardless of the employment rate.

Your Perfect Resume and the Career Discovery Process at the beginning of this book are important steps in the self-directed job campaign. On the following pages are some basic rules and strategies for effective job hunting.

THE HIDDEN JOB MARKET

There is a vast underground marketplace in which over 75 percent of the job openings rise and fall through the dynamics of word of mouth, personal referral, and good luck. They never show up in the daily classifieds. Some rules for tapping into this career information bank:

- **Don't pursue only advertised positions**—be willing to uncover the name, title, and whole address of anyone in *any* organization related to your job target field and call that person for information.

- **Make a list of twenty persons**—relatives, family, friends, past employers, professors, authorities in the field, to whom you could send a personal letter with a few copies of your perfect resume, with the **close** conviction (followed by a phone call) that they could probably forward it to others within your field of interest.

- **Undertake active research** in directories, trade journals, magazines, and books related to your field, once you have clear job targets. Get the names and addresses of at least twenty potential employers *for each job target* and send them a special customized cover letter with your resume.

Individual contact by name is the most effective way into the interviews—without the competition usually provoked when the job gets advertised. The local telephone book yellow pages are a very good source of names of potential employers. Check under two or three related categories. You can get classified directories from other communities in the United States and Canada by a request to your telephone company business office.

Other research sources to use in uncovering the names and addresses of potential employer contacts should include:

- **Business and product directories**—to find out the best directories for you, consult your library or the *Guide to American Directories* (B. Kline & Company, P.O. Box 8530, Coral Springs, FL 33065).

- **Trade and professional associations**—for names and addresses of the most relevant trade associations, consult *National Trade and Professional Associations of the United States and Canada* (Columbia Books Inc., Washington, DC).

- **Back issues of trade publications** in your job target areas—a very valuable source of general and specific information about products, industry trends, and authorities in the field. A comprehensive guide to these journals and other articles and books related to the field can be obtained at the research section of your community or university library.

Organized approach: When you go through the directories and other sources of employer information, have a pack of three-by-five index cards, and list each employer, address, and phone number on a separate card.

GETTING THE INTERVIEW

The purpose of your resume and cover letter is to help you get interviews. There are several proven strategies to assist you in accomplishing this:

- **Call first.** A personal telephone contact with the person with whom you want to have the interview could accelerate the entire process. After you have done your research and obtained the names and addresses and phone numbers of at least twenty potential employers in your field, set aside a period of time (preferably early morning) to place calls to the individuals who can make the hiring decisions.

- **Be sure to know the name and title** of the person you want to reach before initiating the call. Also have a rough idea of what you want to say that will be of interest to him or her. (The answer to the question: *Why should I hire you?*)

- **Have your personal telemarketing campaign organized in advance** so that you can continue to call for at least two hours without having exhausted your reference cards. Then take a couple of hours off to recharge your batteries.

- **Primary objective of call:** To set up an interview directly with the appropriate person.

- **Secondary objective:** To establish personal contact that can be followed up by your resume and cover letter.

- **Resistance:** You will have to slug your way through walls of resistance in this phoning—your resistance (for fear of rejection) and theirs (for fear that you are going to waste their time). The antidote: keep on calling. A string of turndowns is an expected phenomenon in any productive job campaign. As a matter of fact, the whole process looks like this: No No No No No No No No *Yes*. The only way through is to create more Noes faster. Gets you the Yeses that much sooner.

- **Resume/phone call:** This is a second approach, in which you send out your resume and cover letter first, indicating at the conclusion of your letter that you will be calling to set up the interview. Keep good records of when these letters go out and call the recipient *five* days from the date you mailed it. This is designed to time your call for approximately the day after the employer's representative received it. *Make these follow-up calls on schedule.*

- **Be prepared.** Know who the employer is (place, size, employees, branches, brief history). And what they *do:* products, services, markets, competitors, projects, achievements. Know that the quality of your preparation is a direct demonstration of how you would get the job done. Simple but true. Get and read brochures, trade journals, and annual reports. Ask people in the field, competitors, trade associations, and employers.

- **Prompt yourself.** On one side of a three-by-five index card write down five things you want the employer to know about you. On the other side list five questions you want to ask the employer during the interview. Put this card in your pocket or purse, take it with you to the interview, and refer to it.

- **Get feedback.** It's all right to ask the employer if you have the skills she or he is looking for. The worst it will be is no. In which case you get to find out why. Correction furthers the process.

- **Dress like a winner.** It's simple: Let your clothes (hair, weight, makeup, complexion) support your purpose in life. Have your personal presentation demonstrate where you are *aiming*, not where you *are*.

- **Be "outrageous."** Break your old image of yourself. Go after what you want with high intention, determination, and willingness to operate in the work world at an entirely new level.
- **Role-play.** Have a colleague or companion play employer and ask you the five following role-play questions:

    1. What are your strongest abilities?
    2. How do your skills relate to our needs?
    3. What are you looking for in a job?
    4. What would you like to know about us?
    5. Why should we hire you?

- **Critique yourself.** And have your partner do the same.

MAKE MORE MONEY

Please realize that the name of the game is *satisfaction*, not money—work success is having a job that works for you, that lets you be yourself in the work you do. There is no inherent satisfaction in the money you make. Most of us keep our salary hopes two jumps ahead of our earnings throughout our careers regardless of how much we make.

But make more money anyway (if you want to). The more you make, the bigger the jobs you get, and the more fun the game might be. Briefly, here's how:

- Remember that the cardinal economic principle is this: *Money follows value*. The way you make more money is to create more value and to stay with value creation until the results are so good it is impossible not to compensate you, out of the value you create.

Three specific salary negotiating techniques:

1. Always let the employer name the salary figure first. Employers tend to cite higher figures than candidates. Interesting—and true. Don't answer the question "What's the minimum salary you would accept?" Tell the interviewer you're not looking for the minimum and that you will be taking a number of interviews, expect several offers, and will take the one that offers you the best combination of challenge and compensation. Smile nicely as you say it.

2. Whenever a range is named, verbalize the top of the range. Employer: The range is $17,000 to $21,000 per year. You: $21,000 sounds in the right ball park right now.

3. Never accept an offer when it's given. Tell the person who makes it that you appreciate the opportunity, know you can make a contribution, and need to consider it for ten days or so. This shifts the game immediately

into your hand as the employer starts to wonder what else you have been offered. Sometimes offers are increased 10 to 20 percent within a week.

And, again, be courageous. Know it is you who actually let the employer know what you're worth. Be willing to turn down or be turned down if the salary isn't right. Go for it!

A LAST WORD

Thank you for staying with us until the end—the end for us. A beginning for you, we hope, of a new clarity and assertiveness in your resume and in your career search.

Please know that our purpose is strongly behind you, and our support, too. This is a time for all of us to recognize the abundance of opportunity —not necessarily job slots, but true opportunity—for us to make a self-directed contribution to the world in work terms, to get the job done in a way that produces satisfaction and aliveness for ourselves and value for others.

All of us who assisted in this book send you our love and best wishes for a glorious worklife.

About Tom Jackson

Over the past twenty years, Tom Jackson has emerged as one of the nation's leading authorities and commentators on the nature and quality of people's worklives. His place is at the cutting edge of a revolutionary approach to the way people deal with their careers.

Jackson's work takes him deeply into the corporate world of human resources management and career development, as well as to the very pragmatic realities of thousands of individual job seekers and career changers each year in workshops and courses he and his staff conduct.

Other books by Jackson include: *The Hidden Job Market, How To Get The Job You Want in 28 Days, Guerrilla Tactics in the Job Market*. He is also the creator of dozens of training programs and materials in the area of career development and organizational effectiveness, used by corporations, schools, and government.

Jackson's newly developed software, including *The Perfect Resume Computer Kit*™, is used by schools, corporations, and individuals.

Jackson is founder of The Career Development Team and chairman of Equinox Corporation in New York City.

BOOK MARK

*The text of this book was composed in
the typefaces Palatino and Futura
by Crane Typesetting Service, Inc.
West Barnstable, Massachusetts*

*This book was printed
by Courier Book Companies
Kendallville, Indiana*

**BOOK DESIGN BY
PATRICE FODERO**